Bindery 12/00

S

DICTIONARY OF PREHISTORIC INDIAN ARTIFACTS OF THE AMERICAN SOUTHWEST

by Franklin Barnett

PUBLISHED BY NORTHLAND PRESS

S

EDITORIAL STAFF

Project Consultant

Dr. Edward B. Danson

Director, Museum of Northern Arizona, Flagstaff, Arizona

General Editor

Dr. David Hochstettler

Chairman, English Department, Yavapai College, Prescott, Arizona

Archaeological Editors

Dr. John O. Brew

Peabody Professor Emeritus of American Archaeology and Ethnology
Harvard University, Cambridge, Massachusetts

Watson Smith

Archaeologist, Vice-President

Northern Arizona Society of Science and Art, Inc., Flagstaff, Arizona

Contributing Editors

Joan E. Barnett   Dr. Edward Bunney   Nora N. Bunney

Barbara R. Hinkley   Betty C. Schwartz   Cleo Wipff   F. Pershing Wipff

Research Assistants

Joan E. Barnett   Oneita H. Hall

Prehistoric Indian on Cover

Painted by Mr. Konrad Vaeth of Phoenix, Arizona

Copyright © 1973 by Franklin Barnett

All Rights Reserved

FIRST EDITION

ISBN 0–87358–120–2

Library of Congress Catalog Card Number 73–82865

Composed and Printed in the United States of America

To Joan
whose role of
General Factotum of the
entire manuscript
throughout its preparation
was invaluable

As Man today
I greet you, Ancient Brother Man
And point with gratitude
To these the artifacts you made in eons past.
The signature of man's slow rise
Is on each tool, each point, each axe
And we can sense the human impact still.
Who smoked this pipe? Who played this flute?
Who used this hoe? Who threw this spear?
And was it made for enemy — or deer?

As Man today
I kneel upon a mountain circled flat
To feel the ancient ashes yield, and see
A kinship gift which you have left for me.
I grasp within my hand a perfect tool
So long ago chipped carefully from stone,
And know but for the timing of our fates
It might have been my own.
I touch with care its edges keen and fine,
Where once you placed your thumb
There now is mine.

NORA NULL BUNNEY

CONTENTS

FOREWORD

The Franklin Barnetts were introduced to me over seven years ago by one of the archaeological editors of this Dictionary as student archaeologists who were making careful excavation of sites and keeping complete records of their work.

The sites that the Barnetts — Franklin and Joan to their many friends — excavated were carefully selected and were on privately-owned lands. Feeling the need to do a complete job, they also carefully restored the broken artifacts they found. In the process of learning how to restore pottery, Joan Barnett studied ceramics, and she is now one of the best restorers I know. This she did so that she could see the finished pottery as it was known and used by long-dead owners. Each artifact was measured and carefully mapped and finally photographed. Reports were written to the best of Franklin's considerable ability.

The Barnetts began to publish the results of their excavations. *Tonque Pueblo — A Report of Partial Excavation of an Ancient Pueblo IV Indian Ruin in New Mexico* was published in 1969 by the Albuquerque Archaeological Society; *Matli Ranch Ruins — A Report of Excavation of Five Small Prehistoric Indian Ruins of the Prescott Culture in Arizona* was published by the Museum of Northern Arizona (Technical Series No. 10) in 1970; *Lonesome Valley Ruin in Yavapai County, Arizona* was published by the Museum of Northern Arizona (Technical Series No. 13) in 1973. Three more reports await publication.

However, when it came time to describe the artifacts found in all of their excavations, the Barnetts ran into the same troubles that beset all amateurs and most beginning archaeological students. They weren't always quite sure of the proper terms used by archaeologists for a given object.

About two years ago, Joan and Franklin Barnett discussed their problems with archaeological jargon as far as the jargon was connected to the excavation and analysis of Southwestern archaeological sites. They told me that Franklin was thinking of writing an archaeological dictionary that would, with word and picture, help other beginners in the use of proper terminology. I encouraged them, and with their usual enthusiasm, they soon reported that they had found friends who would back the publication of such a dictionary. They purchased camera equipment and Joan began to photograph artifacts from their own collections and later from museum collections in the Southwest.

All books have limits to their scope. Franklin has limited the Dictionary to material found in Southwestern prehistoric sites — open sites or caves. He does not include ceramic wares, weaving, or woven basketry as they are studies within themselves.

The reader of this Dictionary must realize that it attempts to be just that — a compendium of terms used by archaeologists and collectors. Each item has a definition and a photo. The author does not attempt to date all the objects and in many instances, does not go into the cultural connections of the artifact defined.

The photographs used save many pages of writing and, with the terminology, should prove of use to the very persons for whom this book was written, the amateur and the beginning student of archaeology.

Flagstaff, Arizona
1973

Edward B. Danson
Director, Museum of Northern Arizona

PREFACE

This Dictionary is respectfully dedicated to making archaeology more significant to the student by the unification of cultural phases as applied to anthropology. The purpose is to bring under one cover illustrations, descriptions, and uses of the many artifacts of the Indians of the prehistoric American Southwest, hereinafter designated the "Southwest." Every effort is made to bring into focus the varied nomenclature and certain other data concerned with these artifacts. The coverage of such material includes information pertaining to those items recovered by surface survey and excavation, or from dry caves.

Included are resumés of the work, rework, and use of such basic materials as antler, bone, clay (argil), shell, stone, and wood. For the most part, these are the materials from which the prehistoric Indian made his implements: tools, weapons, utensils, ceremonial objects, ornaments and charms. In that long ago era, survival and level of affluence depended upon the degree of ingenuity and skill of individuals and groups.

For comparative purposes, many illustrations of artifacts, or groups of artifacts, are accompanied by scales. The dimensions and weights of various artifacts are frequently noted in the associated text.

As photographs are more apt to portray authentic or precise fabrication detail, this medium of picturing artifacts is used in preference to artists' concept. However, sketches of the *modus operandi* of certain utility artifacts are employed to illustrate use of many of the more involved processes. Additionally, simple line-drawings are also used to illustrate the very few artifacts for which photographs were either not available or unobtainable. The dash lines found between individual photographs of certain pictured artifacts, associate two or more views of that artifact (top, side, obverse, or reverse).

Acknowledgments

In addition to those responsible to a great extent for the "mechanics" and the presentation of this publication as noted under the heading of "Editorial Staff," much is owed to the efforts of the following individuals, and gratitude is also expressed for their guidance, assistance, and general encouragement:

Mrs. Lillian S. Blyth of Prescott, Arizona, made 35 mm slides of each illustration, artifact, and artifact group in the Dictionary. These slides were for use of the Archaeological Editors (Editorial Staff) in conjunction with their archaeological and pictorial editing of the manuscript of this publication.

Dr. and Mrs. Edward Bunney of Wickenburg, Arizona, and Surry, Maine, canvassed the vicinity of Wickenburg for collectors of prehistoric Indian artifacts of the Southwest, who permitted the author to record selected material from their collections for inclusion herein.

Mr. and Mrs. Richard K. Cooke of Wickenburg, Arizona, acted as guides in conducting the author to areas in the vicinities of Wickenburg, Congress, and Aguila, where communal metates and mortars were found grouped in large quantities. These had been used to grind such foods as mesquite beans and cactus fruits by the prehistoric nomadic Indians.

Dr. Edward B. Danson, Director, Museum of Northern Arizona, Flagstaff, Arizona, whose encouragement and enthusiasm toward the Dictionary project when it was first presented as merely an idea, was largely responsible for the incentive to proceed.

Dr. Charles L. Douglas and Miss Margaret Jean Whitman, of the Center for Man and Environment, Prescott College, Prescott, Arizona, provided information and classification of bone artifacts made from basic faunal remains in the Southwest.

Dr. Emil W. Haury, Professor of Anthropology at the University of Arizona, Tucson, Arizona, classified discs and spindle whorls made from stone, clay material, and potsherds.

Mr. and Mrs. William E. Hinkley of Phoenix, Arizona, were, in a measure, co-originators of the idea of a dictionary such as this. They contacted collectors in the vicinity of Phoenix and Casa Grande, Arizona, obtaining permission for the author to record selected items from their prehistoric Indian artifacts' collections for publication herein. Additionally, they are the exclusive underwriters of this entire publication.

Mr. Gomer Jones of Gomer Jones Dodge Co., Prescott, Arizona, furnished transportation for off-highway travel to photograph and record artifacts in remote areas.

Mr. Michael W. Knapp, student conchologist of Los Angeles, California, identified and classified sea shells recovered from ruins in the Southwest.

Mr. Edward F. Miller of Prescott, Arizona, is the contributor of certain detail photographs of artifacts, as indicated by the lower case underscored letter "m" under specific photographs throughout this publication.

Dr. Carleton B. Moore, Director, Center for Meteorite Studies, Arizona State

University, Tempe, Arizona, obtained the Microprobe Laboratory report of the metallic nodules covered under "Decorative Stone, Unworked."

Mr. and Mrs. Merlyn Talbot of Camp Verde, Arizona, contacted the collectors of prehistoric Indian artifacts located in Camp Verde and environs, and obtained permission for the author to record selected material from their collections.

Prescott, Arizona
1973

Franklin Barnett

Prescott, Arizona
1973

Franklin Barnett

GUIDE TO THE
USE OF THIS DICTIONARY

All artifacts have been entered in alphabetical order. If two or more variant names exist to identify the same article, the description and spelling of its most common and frequent usage are given first. Commonly used synonyms and common obsolete terms are also listed in their alphabetical position with cross-reference.

Primary nomenclature of artifacts is shown in bold face capital and lower case letters. Secondary nomenclature or variations in the nomenclature of basic artifacts is shown in bold face lower case letters, and is set parenthetically from the primary nomenclature.

Artifacts are sometimes made from several different kinds of material. In such cases, each is described separately under subtitles of the material involved.

Spanish, Latin, and Indian terms are only used to the extent that they may elaborate or clarify a particular explanation.

For convenience of the user, various measurements contained throughout the text are given both in feet and inches (or fractions thereof), and in the metric system. When dimensions are given as either inclusive or approximate, they apply to objects or separate items in groups of objects which were measured by the author or from published reports. When a dimension is given for a specific item, it applies to that item only. In most cases where pertinent, artifacts can be measured from the scale which accompanies the illustration. Weights are expressed in pounds and/or a decimal fraction thereof.

A glossary is included which gives explanations of certain words and phrases as used in this Dictionary.

Noted throughout the text and under certain photographs of artifacts or groups of artifacts are capital and/or lower case letters, and Arabic numerals. The indicated coding of specific artifacts or groups of pictured artifacts denotes the following:

Capital letter "A, B, etc" indicates a cross-reference letter between certain descriptive textual material, and the corresponding lettered artifact in the associated photograph. Certain artifacts (indicated by capital letters), additionally contain lower case letters in conjunction with the capital letter. These signify sub-detail versions of the specific artifact indicated.

Arabic numerals located to the lower left of certain pictured artifacts identify that item as belonging in the collection of the corresponding Arabic numbered museum, publication, or individual listed under "Contributors."

Lower case underscored letter "t" found beneath a photograph of an artifact indicates that the particular photo was taken by Helga Teiwes (see *Museums,* Item 1, under "Contributors").

Lower case underscored letter "g" found beneath a photograph of an artifact indicates that the particular photo was taken by Marc Gaede (see *Museums,* Item 3, under "Contributors").

Lower case underscored letter "b" found beneath a photograph of an artifact indicates that the particular photo was taken by Mrs. Blyth (see *Publication Credits* under "Contributors").

Lower case underscored letter "m" found beneath a photograph of an artifact indicates that the particular photo was taken by Mr. Miller (see *Acknowledgements* under the Preface).

All photographs of artifacts not otherwise credited were taken by Mrs. Joan E. Barnett of Prescott, Arizona.

To derive maximum efficiency from use of this Dictionary, each user is urged to read the *Introduction* on the following pages. Answers to many questions of a general nature will be found there.

INTRODUCTION

SCOPE

This Dictionary concerns itself with the artifacts of the Indians of the American Southwest in the period prior to recorded history. This period terminated in A.D. 1540 when the Spanish invaders and their allies brought in their padres and chroniclers. The territory designated as the "Southwest" is interpreted by this Dictionary to consist of Southeastern Utah, Southwestern Colorado, and the region within the political boundaries of the combined States of Arizona and New Mexico.

Every effort has been made to include representative artifacts of a workaday, projectile and weapon, charm and ornamental, and ceremonial nature. Such items, whether made from antler, bone, clay, lithic (stone), shell, or wood material are pictured and described. Further facts having to do with cultures, dates, and references are included with respect to some artifacts of particular significance.

The artifacts pictured herein are typical examples of the depicted item, and are for use as guides for identification purposes. There are over 250 different major types of artifacts included. Minor variations of most artifacts are far too numerous to detail. This publication is a compilation of the nomenclature, identification, use, and general information on artifacts of the prehistoric Indian in the American Southwest.

This Dictionary of artifacts does not include data concerning ceramic wares, matting, blankets, weaving, or woven basketry. Information regarding these kinds of artifacts is covered in the many reports of excavations and dry cave exploration, and other special publications concerning such artifacts of the Southwest.

Much of the material contained herein is based upon information researched in various archaeological reports and records, and in some cases, information merely suggested in such reports. Further investigation at museums and study of collections was necessary for controversial subject matter found throughout researched material.

PREHISTORIC CULTURAL PERIODS

The basic Indian cultures have existed in the Southwest since long before the Christian era. Upon their arrival in the expanse of the great American Southwest,

1

the prehistoric Indians were faced with little of an inviting nature. Far and wide, and except for rugged mountains to the west and north, the vista presented very little beyond barren wastes. True, in some areas of the Southwest, more generally in the mountainous regions and in the meadows near the base of these mountains, game seemed to abound. But to capture and kill these animals presented a problem. Heavily meated animals such as antelope, deer, mountain sheep, bear, and even rabbits were swift afoot and difficult to approach. Meat was a main staple for these early Indians, and, except for some smaller animals, rodents, and birds, procurement presented a difficulty.

Thus, these people who were new to the country, were forced to develop ways of survival — or perish. That they learned quickly is attested to by the multiple cultures which developed from the basic cultural groups throughout the Southwest, and the quantities of cultural materials they left.

There is no effort here to detail the history of the periods, but only to present a resumé to indicate certain highlights for orientation and comparative purposes. The history of the prehistoric Indians has been fully worked out by scientific investigations, and covered in detail by advanced students of these early peoples.

"Prehistoric People" is contrued to mean the four major Indian cultures of the early Southwest — the base for the many cultural offshoots, or branches, from these. There is a considerable overlapping of the four major cultures, as there is of the cultural offshoots.

Within the Southwest area with which this Dictionary is concerned, the general geographic distribution of these cultures (see map) is as follows:

> In the north central portion were the Anasazi. The early Anasazi were called the Basketmakers, A.D. 1 to 750, and the later Anasazi were called the Pueblo Indians, A.D. 700 to date.

> In the south central portion was the Mogollon Culture. The early period, as early as B.C. 10,000, is called the Desert Culture. The later period, about B.C. 5,000, is called the Cochise Culture. The period pre B.C. 300 to A.D. 1000 is the Mogollon Culture.

> West of the Mogollon Culture the Hohokam Culture existed pre A.D. 1 to 1400.

> To the west of the above cultures the Patayan Culture came into existence about B.C. 4,000, but the culture dated circa A.D. 200 to 1300 is best known.

In addition to artifacts from the four basic cultures, the A.D. 1540 Dictionary terminal date permits the inclusion of artifacts from the Indians who represent branches of the four basic cultures, and the artifacts from the Apache, Navajo, and other tribes who came into the Southwest from the North during prehistoric times.

In this dictionary the term "pre-Columbian" (based upon Columbus's arrival date in 1492 on the east coast of America) is not used because the Southwest Indian cultures were free of non-Indian influences until 48 years later in 1540,

2

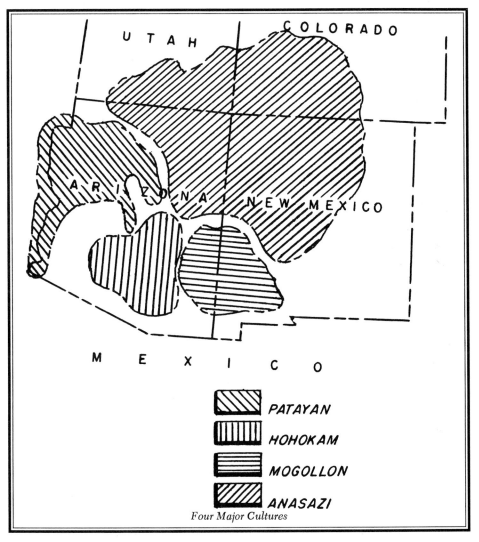

Four Major Cultures

PATAYAN
HOHOKAM
MOGOLLON
ANASAZI

when the Spanish first appeared in numbers in the Southwest. As time went on, the artifacts made by the descendants of the prehistoric Indian cultures with which we are concerned began to be somewhat influenced by the Spanish occupation. Such artifacts are not included here.

The complex of individual or unrelated groups of the Indians designated as "cultures" refers to those groups located in geographic areas within the over-all time periods indicated above. The periods of existence of the cultures are dated by ceramic analysis, dendrochronology (tree-ring), Carbon 14, stratigraphic analysis, and other kinds of laboratory tests (see Michels, 1973; and Smiley, *et al*, 1953).

The greatest development of the prehistoric Indian in affluence, the arts, larger and better living quarters and conditions, and elaborate ceremonial life and equipage was from circa A.D. 1050 to 1300. The greatest surge being about the mid-13th Century. The end of the period in the Northern Southwest was probably hastened by the great 20-year drouth of the later 1200's, which ended circa 1300.

Generally, the period dating from circa A.D. 1350 to 1540, includes the decadence of some of the cultures and the flowering of Awatovi, Hawikuh, Sikyatki, and many of the Rio Grande Pueblos during the later 14th and early 15th Centuries. This period also included the advent of the Spanish (1540) into the Southwest, which caused a change in the way of life for the early Indian, and, as a consequence, his arts and crafts.

WORK AND REWORK OF BASIC MATERIALS

Materials at the disposal of these prehistoric Indians might be considered quite limited. However, to these peoples, a whole new world opened and lay before them. Even though much of this country is desert, the early Indians, semi-nomadic at first, became farmers and local hunters and settled in masonry or adobe houses and towns (pueblos). They produced large quantites of numerous kinds of artifacts — tools, implements, weapons, ceramic wares, *et al*, which were utilized in their struggle for existence.

Each material such as antler, bone, clay, shell, stone, and wood utilized by the prehistoric Indian was applied to whatever use was best suited. Various materials were modified according to necessity, and were altered (worked) to increase convenience of their use. Work on basic materials was performed as noted in paragraphs concerned with the particular material indicated.

The prehistoric Indians not only worked with the materials noted above, but utilized fragments of broken lithic and ceramic artifacts, as well. Additionally, clay (pottery material) was used to make items of an ornamental, utilitarian, or ceremonial nature.

It is not the intent of this Dictionary to enter into the detailed mechanics of the fabrication, or even detailed work or rework of materials. Information involving the use of certain specific prehistoric tools and *modus operandi* is included to give the reader a general understanding of the basic efforts involved in the shaping and drilling of artifacts created by the ingenious Indian artisans of the Southwest.

Many of the processes noted were also employed during the rework of certain artifacts, when another use of a piece was desired.

BASIC MATERIALS

ANTLER: Antlers were used far less than bone because they were relatively soft and spongy and so less satisfactory to use for many implements. The tine,

4

itself, was often a ready-made tool. A limitation of usage was that antler material would not withstand continued implemental use. The strength of antler material, which actually is the horn or a branch of such horn of an animal of the deer family, is governed by the proximity of the tine to the skull. The "brow" antler is the toughest, being located closer to the animal's skull. The "bay" and "royal" antlers are next, and the "surroyal," or the farthest tine or prong of the antler is last, and so the least tough.

Because of the non-durable quality of antler material, many of these artifacts have been almost impossible to recover intact, even when found.

New and rather advanced recovery and preservation techniques for the retention of perishable materials such as antler, wood, and some shell artifacts are being developed, and should be followed closely.

Probably because the tip of the tine, itself, provided a ready-made tool, there was very little work, if any, required to make it useful. Most tines were snapped off from the horn and used as they were. Others were abraded smooth at the break point. Still others had been removed by transverse sawing. The tip end of antler artifacts are either round, beveled, or pointed. These all show evidence of having been used for flaking, rubbing, or light forms of abrasion.

Some tines were split lengthwise, and the edges and inside spongy portion abraded flat, or the spongy part even removed. These were used as battens during weaving operations. For this kind of work, the ends were rounded and beveled.

BONE: In general, bones (bird or other faunal remains) were worked in various ways to make items of just about any kind — workaday implements, musical instruments (wind or percussion), ornaments, charms, and ceremonial objects. All bone substance had to be worked in some manner before it could be used.

That the prehistoric Indian utilized just about every part of any bone from faunal remains (except in some cases the proximal and/or distal joints), is evidenced by the many kinds of bone artifacts which have been recovered. These items range from utility to those of an ornamental nature.

Bones from birds, rodents, and mammals, which were used, would represent the kinds one would find in the Southwest today. They would be the inhabitants of the Sonoran and Chihuahuan Life Zones, and have a wide distribution throughout the Southwest.

Some of the more common bones used would include those from the turkey, hawk, cottontail rabbit, jackrabbit, pocket gopher, woodrat, prairie dog, rock squirrel, bobcat, coyote, dog, gray fox, deer, and antelope. While the bones of carnivores were utilized along with others, there is no way of knowing whether these animals were hunted for their hides, their meat, or for both.

Because of the nature of the material, bone (except for large mammal bones) was comparatively easy to work into whatever item was desired.

To obtain various lengths of tubular bones, or to remove the proximal or distal ends, a bird, rodent, or large mammal bone was sawed in transverse section with

5

a hard notched stone saw. Gravers were also used to score small tubular rodent and bird bone, which was then easily broken along the encircling mark. Joint ends thus removed were discarded.

Holes were started in much the same manner, *i.e.*, by transverse sawing into the bone. When the hole was started, it was then drilled or reamed with a stone drill point or reamer to the diameter desired.

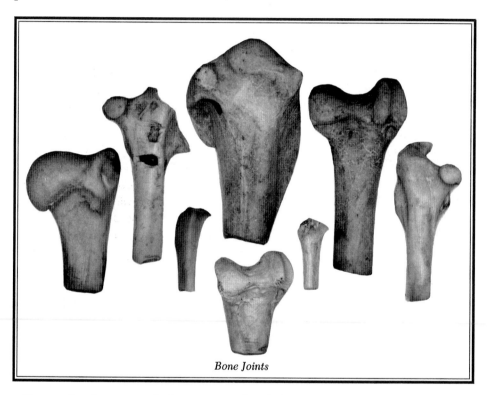

Bone Joints

Raw ends of cut or split bone were abraded smooth with handheld abrading stones of sandstone, slate, and even vesicular basalt. Practically any stone possessing abrasive qualities was used.

To produce a pointed end, a bone was worked and/or sharpened on a sharpening stone or slab, sometimes called an "awl pointer." These were generally made from fine-grained sandstone or other similar abrasive stone.

Awls, needles, or other shaft-like bone items were often made from heavy tubular bones from mammals. The bone was split longitudinally, then the segment was abraded smooth and pointed as desired.

Many joint ends of awls, which were not removed, were carved to resemble birds, animals or spherical knobs. Some were carved spatulate shape, with teeth (notches) or other unusual forms. Many awls and other bone implements were graved with various motifs such as simple geometrics, encircling spirals, or grooves.

Many bone items, such as tubular beads or shafts of one sort or another, were polished with smooth abraders such as grooved polishing stones. Ashes, pumice, and other powdered abrasives were also used. In some cases the kind of bone used to make a given artifact is impossible to identify. This is because the work of shaping the bone piece removed all identifying features.

CLAY: Included are the unique hand-molded artifacts which were made from clay material, and which were both unfired and fired. These artifacts do not include ceramic wares (vessels). While workmanship may vary from one culture to another, most of the items noted are comparatively crude. This condition makes it difficult to determine "typical" pieces. In general, the fired fetishes, figurines, and spindle whorls might be considered less carefully made than other hand-molded items, as they are usually rough, unfinished, and often overfired as well.

Many items, hand-molded from different clay materials, were fired in the same manner as ceramic vessels. Most of these are quite crude, and, except for the spherical beads and spool-shaped spindle whorls, seem to be symbolic in nature rather than efforts to make miniature reproductions of human or animal forms.

Artifacts made from unfired clay material are quite scarce. This is because such material would generally disintegrate through the centuries, whether on the surface or underground (damp/dry earth condition of the fill), and be reincorporated in the earth.

POTSHERDS: While potsherds are not considered a basic material, it is a material from which many kinds of artifacts were made. Such sherds resulted from broken decorated and utility ceramic wares. Every culture in the Southwest utilized sherds of ceramic wares for some sort of secondary artifact item. The rework on many of these artifacts is quite well done, while others indicate only a minimum amount of effort.

Rework of sherds into a usable item such as a gaming piece, charm, pendant, spindle whorl, etc., was performed in one of two ways, or both. Pieces were rough-shaped by chipping the edges, then finished by abrading at 90° to the surface of the piece. Other items were abraded to the desired shape without the benefit of edge chipping. Items were perforated as desired.

SHELL: Almost any kind of shell was utilized, usually for the making of ornaments and charms. Shell did not lend itself as a material for utility items because of the fragility of the shell material.

Except for the gastropoda (snail — univalve, *Family Helicidae*) which are terrestrial and not marine, shells were obtained either by trade with Indians from the Gulf of Mexico, the Gulf of California, or the Pacific Coast, or by excursions to those areas. That such trade was extensive is evidenced by the number of shell artifacts recovered from ruins in the Southwest.

7

The types of shells used were practically unlimited. Worked items from valves of bivalves, and univalve shells recovered attest to this. To enumerate the shell used to make charm and ornament items would be an overwhelming task.

It is suggested that authentic guides to kind of sea shells and their localities of origin, such as Abbott's *Sea Shells of the World* (1962), be consulted for identification when specific shell artifacts are involved.

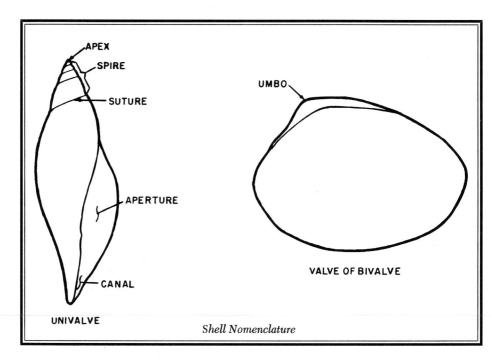

Shell Nomenclature

All shells had to be worked at least to some extent, before they could be worn as ornaments or utilized as charms.

Single valves of bivalve shells were abraded on the umbo, or beak portion, near the hinge area to make a through hole for stringing as a pendant or drop. Some larger valves of bivalve shells were shaped rectangularly or in variations of this shape by cutting or abrasion, then drilled and worn as pendants. Often the centers of the valves of bivalve shells were cut out leaving the encircling edge to produce a ring or bracelet, depending upon the size of the shell used. Some shells were worked into charms by graving. Some of these were also drilled for wearing in a necklace.

Univalve shells were worked in several ways. The most common was the making of beads from the small olivella shells. The apex of the spire was abraded off to make a hole for stringing. Some olivella shells were abraded, additionally, at the opening of the canal. This produced a cylindrically-shaped

8

bead. Many univalve shells (though generally olivella) are recovered in their original, or unworked condition. Examination of most of these reveal that the canal opening contains compacted sand or other particulate matter wedged into the opening. Unable to remove the obstructions without damaging the shell, they could not be strung, and so were not used.

Many of the larger univalve shells (conus, screw, etc) had the spire cut or abraded off at the base, which left a bell-shaped piece, sometimes called a "tinkler." A hole was sawed or abraded transversely into the flange at the canal end of the shell for stringing. Some conus and similar type shells had the apex of the spire abraded off to make a hole for stringing.

STONE: Stone of every kind and description had the widest use of all materials. As has been noted, stone, generally from the locality concerned, was used for tool, weapon, utensil, charm, and ornament phases of a prehistoric Indian's way of life. He was able to work even hard stone into objects necessary to further his existence. Semi-precious gem stone such as turquoise, jadeite, jet, and even argillite (though argillite is not considered a gem stone), or other semi-precious gem stones which could be found locally, were used for the making of ceremonial, charm, or ornamental items.

Of all the kinds of semi-precious gem stones available to the prehistoric Indians and worked by them, turquoise was the favorite, even as it is a favorite gem stone of the Indians today. The Spaniards upon entering the Southwest (1540), found turquoise ornaments in great quantities among the Indians (see Color Plate I, Item 2, p. 10). Though most charms and ornaments were carved from argillite, turquoise was still the number one material used for ornaments of personal adornment such as beads, pendants, inlay, drops, and an almost endless list of such items. This was not only because of its attractive appearance, but also, possibly, because turquoise rates only 5-6 on the Mohs Hardness Scale, indicating it was easily worked. Turquoise has, when polished, an attractive range of color and lustre — colors which range from sky blue to dark blue to bluish-green (see Color Plate I, Item 2, p. 10).

The peoples of many cultures either traveled great distances to procure turquoise, or traded for chunks with nomadic Indians they encountered (see Color Plate I, Item 1, p. 10), and worked these chunks to their fancy. This condition was caused by the fact that good turquoise was only found in certain localities scattered throughout the American Southwest (see Sec. "Mines and Prospects," in Pogue, *Turquois*, 1972). Modern locations of sources may vary generally be classified by color-grade as follows: shades of a greenish-blue (called Blue Gem) from areas in Nevada; a true turquoise color (called Villa Grove) from Colorado; pale blue (sometimes called Cerrillos Blue) from New Mexico; and very deep to light blue with heavy dark matrix (called Morenci or Bisbee) from Arizona. The publication *Turquois* (see Sec. "Stone and Mineral," p. 228) is recommended for more detailed study of turquoise.

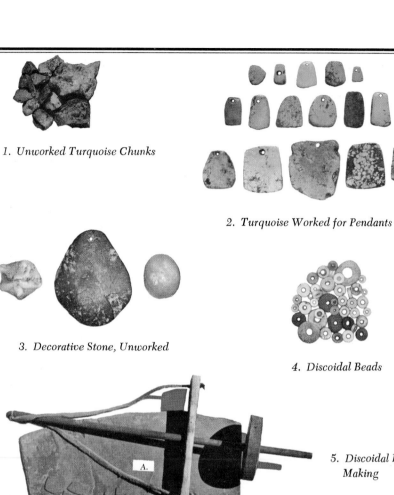

1. *Unworked Turquoise Chunks*

2. *Turquoise Worked for Pendants*

3. *Decorative Stone, Unworked*

4. *Discoidal Beads*

5. *Discoidal Bead Making*

A. *Pump Drill*
B. *Cut Squares*
C. *Abraded Layers of Argillite*
D. *Hole Drilled in One Side*
E. *Complete Hole in Cut Squares*
F. *Finished Beads*
G. *Bead Polishing Slab*
H. *Drill Points*

6. *Sets*

7. *Turquoise Set in Pendants*

Color Plate I   Use of Gem and Semi-Precious Stone

10

Slate, shale, jadeite, and schist were sometimes used for ornaments; and sandstone, schist, and other stones were generally used for utility items. Hard or tough stone such as agate, flint, petrified wood, chert, jasper, and basalt were used for the making of projectiles, weapons, drills, gravers, and other tools. Vesicular basalt, granite, rhyolite, limestone, and locally available stone of this nature were used for utility items as required.

Because of its toughness, the prehistoric Indian found many uses for basalt. This is an extrusive igneous rock which runs to dark colors of gray to black (sometimes greenish), and is a fine grained rock which had been blown out, often in desert areas, onto the earth's surface by volcanic action. It was formed by the cooling of the once hot mass of rock-forming material called "magma." In desert areas the material, often referred to as "malpais" or "basaltic lava," may have a limey crust over the exterior surface, which is often covered with a superficial gloss coating called "desert varnish." Basalt was used for axes, mauls, metates, manos, abraders, and many more utilitarian implements.

Vesicular basalt is a porous hard heavy volcanic rock (see "basalt," above). The small openings (or vugs) were produced by gas or air bubbles which formed in the molten rock at the time of the volcanic extrusive action. As has been previously noted concerning basalt, vesicular basalt was also widely used by the prehistoric Indian. The material was obtainable in many areas, and was found in colors of red, brown-red, gray, and black. Vesicular basalt was used for the making of metates, mortars, manos, small containers, pestles, abraders, mauls, and many other workaday implements.

In most cases, the kind of stone employed for the making of certain artifacts was governed by the stone available in the vicinity. Often such material as semiprecious gem stone, found in one locality, was traded to the inhabitants from another for hard flint, petrified wood, agate, and so on. The student may become frustrated by not being able to identify the material from which certain lithic artifacts were made, or their locality of origin. It is suggested that authentic rock and gem stone guides such as Zim, 1964, be consulted for the identity of such materials.

An example of a series of common materials, all of a similar nature and appearance and difficult to identify when made into small artifacts, might be said to be clay, schist, shale, and slate.

All kinds of stone used by the prehistoric Indian were shaped by chipping or flaking, pecking, abrasion, or drilling to form the item desired. The amount and kind of work were governed by the purpose of the item and the stone being worked (see "Shaping" below).

UNWORKED STONE: These are usually waterworn stones or fieldstones which did not require work, and are unmodified except from use. Some artifacts falling into this category are polishing stones, floor and wall polishers, shaft polishers, grinding stones, hammerstones, abrading slabs, tabular slabs (used for many purposes), and many others.

These unworked artifacts are differentiated from "Unworked Decorative Stones" in that they show some evidence of having been used as workaday implements. Such evidence might be one or more faceted areas from abrasion or pounding, marks from pecking, one or more grooves, or other man-made marks.

Large immobile boulders or other large stone masses also fall into the "unworked" category. Such items as fixed axe sharpeners (large handy boulders with the right abrasive qualities), mortars and metates (oversized boulders or outcroppings, stone creek beds, and stone ledges used in communal grinding efforts), all are unworked except from use.

DESERT VARNISH: Desert varnish, also referred to as "patination," is a lustrous brown to black veneer found on both exposed desert stones and artifacts. Such "varnish" is caused by chemical contents from the decomposition of certain lichen, which becomes oxidized and so produces, through exposure to sunlight, a glossy surface (Rogers, 1966.35, and 136-137).

WOOD: Except for roof beams, roof supports, and the like, artifacts made from wood have been recovered by excavation only to a limited degree. This is because of the alternate damp/dry conditions of the earth, which would cause decomposition of small wood pieces. Most of the wooden artifacts recovered in the Southwest have been found in dry caves. However, improvement in excavating techniques, handling of charred specimens, and preservation systems will lead to more extensive recovery of wooden artifacts in the future.

Undoubtedly wood (other than that used for construction purposes), was used for items of a utility and ornamental nature, much the same as bone. The same methods were used in fashioning wood splinters into useful objects as those which were employed in working on bone.

Besides wood used for construction purposes and slivers for awls, twigs were stripped of their bark and used for weaving of matting, woven into toys or even fetishes. Willow was especially utilized for the making of toys and other objects.

SHAPING: The shaping of any material was the process of producing a desired form from chunks of various kinds of material of an indefinite shape and size. Such efforts were performed by chipping, flaking, pecking, and abrasion — or a combination of all of these. That the prehistoric Indian was a master-craftsman in using only the materials at hand, such as antler, bone, clay, shell, stone, and wood, is evidenced by the fine workmanship found on ornaments and charms, as well as his workaday utensils, weapons, or other implements.

While most cultures of a given period were on a parity of workmanship with their neighbors, some excelled in one phase or another. Examples of excellence of advanced craftsmanship (comparatively) might be said to be the delicately fashioned ornaments and charms of the Hohokam; the fine draftsmanship exhibited on the ceramic wares of the Mimbres; the lithic work of the Cibola; the highly involved and complicated design elements on the St. Johns and Tularosa ceramic wares; the use of a true glaze by the potters of the upper Rio Grande, and, long before them, the Basketmaker III (A.D. 500-750) potters of Southwestern Colorado.

CHIPPING: Chipping is the process utilizing hammer percussion for the breaking off of small fragments from the edge of stone, generally from larger chips or chunks. This is one method in making arrowpoints, drills, gravers, scrapers, and reamers. It is often followed with edge pressure retouch flaking. Additionally, larger items such as deflectors, covers (jar lids), support blocks, and many artifacts made from tabular stone are shaped by the chipping process.

FLAKING: Flaking, a shaping process of removing small fragments of stone by the use of controlled pressure, generally serves the same purpose and performs the same function in shaping of similar objects as chipping. It is sometimes difficult, if not impossible, to differentiate between the results of the two shaping methods.

PECKING: This is a percussion process of striking the flat surface of a stone with repeated series of sharp blows, using a harder stone than that being worked, and thus removing small bits from the surface. While this may seem a laborious process of shaping, it is noted that such artifacts as axes, mauls, paint dishes, various shaped manos, metates, abraders, grinding stones, pounders, spheres, and many more too numerous to mention were shaped in this manner.

ABRASION AND POLISHING: Abrading was performed on bone, shell, shaped potsherds, and stone, by using coarse-to-fine grades of sandstone, or other abrasive stone, antler, potsherds, or other substances as required for the job at hand. Stone items which had been previously shaped, generally by pecking, were often abraded and polished to give a smooth surface or contour. Such items as many kinds of axes, mauls, spheres, paint dishes, charms, ornaments, and fetishes, were dressed in this manner.

DRILLING AND REAMING: Perforating by drilling or reaming into different materials was an operation performed by all cultures. There are several methods which were undoubtedly employed by these peoples. Drilling operations were probably aided by the use of various pulverized and wetted abrasives such as sandstone, pumice, oxides, etc. Basic drilling (subsequent to a possible "start" by transverse sawing with a hard stone implement containing notches) was probably performed by one of the following three methods:

    (a) a drill point was attached to the end of a straight shaft, and when placed in position, was rotated back and forth rapidly between the palms of the hands by rubbing them together.

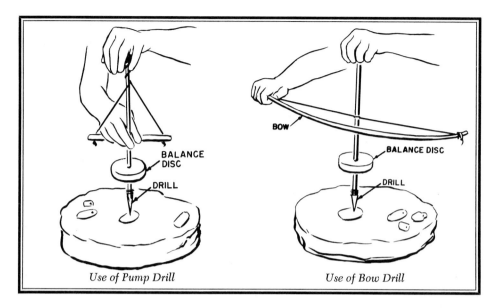

Use of Pump Drill   Use of Bow Drill

(b) a pump drill consisted of a shaft with a drill point attached, a balance disc, and a small cross bar attached to the top of the shaft by thongs extending to the ends of the cross bar. The shaft was turned to "wind up" the thongs, then the bar was pressed down rapidly and released upward. The vertical pumping motion, which wound and rewound the thongs, was continued as rapidly as possible until the hole was completed.

(c) a third method was by use of a "bow" drill. Here, again, the drill point was attached to a shaft. The string of a small bow was wound once around the shaft, and the bow pulled rapidly back and forth.

In the operations (b & c) above, generally a small spherical stone piece, called a "shaft holder," was used to steady the upper end of the shaft, to permit its rotation.

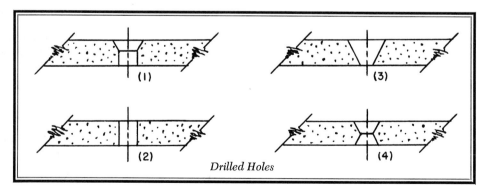

Drilled Holes

There seem to have been four types of holes drilled in various materials:

1. holes which were either pilot-drilled, or countersunk (conical), either before or after the through hole was drilled;

2. holes which were drilled through and which show only one diameter;

3. holes which were drilled from one side of the material with a bevel-pointed drill, which produced a full-beveled hole; and

4. beveled holes which were usually drilled from the outside of the item, but are also drilled from the inside (biconically). The effect of a counter-sunk hole was attained by use of a short or blunt taper-pointed drill.

The very small holes found in charms and ornaments (especially small discoidal beads), were drilled by use of the very sharp points of yucca leaves, spines of agave or cactus, or even small tough reeds, and a wetted abrasive.

The process of reaming was a rotating hand-worked operation using a tough drill-shaped stone. Reamers were usually made to perform a specific enlarging or

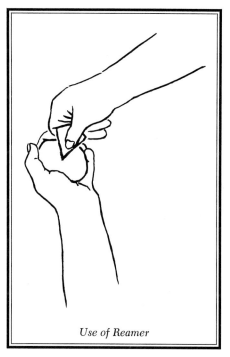

Use of Reamer

shaping operation. This finishing tool (similar to a drill) contained a cutting edge, (see Reamer).

DICTIONARY OF ARTIFACTS

Without written records, the cultures of the prehistoric peoples of the South-west are judged by the craftsmanship of the material culture left by each of them. The legacy of the material remains left by them is a challenge of recon-struction of their lives to every student of archaeology, ethnology, and anthro-pology. As has been previously noted, certain cultures excelled in the design motifs and draftsmanship applied to their ceramic wares, while others made beautifully carved charms and ornaments. Still others are judged by their archi-tectural details of construction, and others by the symmetry of their workaday implements. In the matter of projectiles, none seemed to outdo the other. This because none of the prehistoric Indians of the Southwest had progressed beyond the bow and arrow, spear, or axe era.

In the matter of affluence, many cultures seemed to have devoted more time and effort to the making of various ceramic wares, implements, and so on, and as a result produced more and finer material. Others only produced a minimum number of utensils, and tools, and these were usually of an inferior quality. Com-parisons quickly distinguish products of master craftsmanship from items which were produced merely to meet requirements of daily living. Producers of these latter artifacts might be considered "poor," and seemed to lack progressiveness as well as possessions.

The artifacts covered in the following pages comprise a general cross-section of material from various cultures in the Southwest. No effort has been made to up-grade or "glorify" any one culture's products over another because of work-manship, decorative ability, or any other comparative basis; thus, an impartial and factual viewpoint is presented.

There is no basis for determining the quantity or numerical count of the pre-historic Indian artifacts recovered in the American Southwest. The numbers do not follow any fixed pattern, whether by areas, cultures, surface, or excavation. Some artifacts, such as arrowpoints, hammerstones, drills, beads, scrapers, grind-ing stones, and pendants, are recovered in comparatively large numbers through-out certain areas of residence (sites) of the early inhabitants of the Southwest. Other artifacts, such as charms, ornaments, ceremonial objects, and fetishes, are, when compared to those listed above, more scarce. It is quite obvious that items of a workaday variety were far more plentiful than those of a sacred, ornamental,

19

or ceremonial nature, primarily because a great many more were required for daily use.

The general areas of recovery of only odd or unusual artifacts are noted. This is for the benefit of those interested in comparative measures between material culture and areas from which such material came.

While every effort is made to classify groupings for each specific series of related artifacts, the purpose, use, or even nomenclature of a few artifacts (more often ceremonial) cannot be identified with absolute certainty. This is primarily because of a lack of association with known items of today. In such cases, inferred use has been postulated, but for the sake of discussion, is sometimes restricted to detailed description.

In some cases it is impossible to identify the use of a few artifacts. Rather than to ignore such material, these are included after the letter "Z" under the heading "Artifacts of Unknown Usage."

Abrader: These were made from almost any available stone, and occasionally other materials, containing the desired abrasive qualities. Such material, generally unshaped except from use, was used for fine grinding, abrasion or polishing operations. The pieces pictured, recovered from ruins north of Albuquerque, New Mexico, include a chunk of quartz-crystal, petri-

Abraders

fied antler, a small segment of abalone shell, and small chunks of various grades of fine-grained sandstone, all shaped from use.

Also included in this category are antler tines which are abraded flat across the ends. These probably were used as fleshers, mild abraders, or even polishers (see Flesher, Antler).

Abrader, Shaped: These small shaped abraders were made from fine-grained red sandstone. Each was dressed smooth on all sides with the exception of (A), which contains a series of shallow grooves on each linear side, and a deep groove in one end. The piece (A) was also painted a brown-red (probably hematite) on one grooved edge. Each of the pieces measure 1½ to 1¾ inches (3.81 to 4.44 cm) long by 1-1/16 to 1⅛ inches (2.70 to 2.86 cm) wide by a half inch (1.27 cm) thick. These shaped abraders were undoubtedly used for fine or delicate abrasion work.

Shaped Abraders

Abrading Slab: Abrading slabs (sometimes called a "**bead polishing stone**," or an "**abrading tablet**") were flat irregular unshaped waterworn rocks, slabs of tabular sandstone, slate, rhyolite, or just about any tabular-type stone containing the desired abrasive quality. The edges of some tabular pieces were rough-chipped to shape the piece generally rectangular, but sometimes merely irregular.

The waterworn slabs (A) are sometimes diffi-

cult to identify, as one or both flat or slightly concaved surfaces might show only scant indications of wear by abrasion.

The tablet (B) is an excellent example of a shaped fine-grained sandstone abrasive slab. The piece was abraded smooth on both sides, and contains a smooth encircling beveled edge. The two holes were probably used with pins to secure the piece in place when in use. This abrasive slab was recovered to the northwest of Quemado, New Mexico.

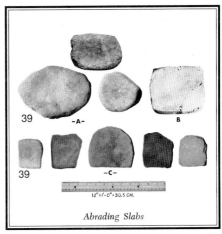

Abrading Slabs

The smaller slabs (C) were rough-shaped by chipping. They are different grades of sandstone (fine to coarse), and were probably used for small abrading jobs. There is no particular shape, but each piece was abraded smooth on both sides.

Most of these artifacts are identified by at least one side showing evidence of having been worked smooth or slightly concaved by the abrasion of small flat items, and sometimes by the chipped edges of the piece.

Many of these slabs were used as passive (fixed position) abraders on which various small flat artifacts were abraded smooth. However, smaller abrading slabs were active (hand-held) abraders, but served the same purpose.

Abrading Stone: Unworked abrading stones (sometimes called "**whetstones**") were active (hand-held) stones with high abrasive qualities. They were used to sharpen edges of tools of stone or bone weapons, or to abrade areas of stone, bone, or shell to a desired contour or smoothness.

Some larger stones, even boulders, sometimes called passive-type abraders, were used from a fixed position. Such stones or boulders were

Abrading Tablet : Arm and Leg Ornament

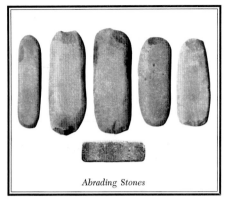

Abrading Stones

generally utilized for communal sharpening operations.

Abrading Tablet, see Abrading Slab

Amulet, see Charm

Animal Figurine, see Fetish

Anvil: Anvils (sometimes called "**grooved hand-stones**") were used in the "paddle and anvil" method of ceramic vessel fabrication by many cultures. This method involved the making of a vessel by the build-up of thin coils of pottery material to the general shape desired. The anvil was held against the inside of the vessel wall while the outside surface was patted smooth to the desired thickness with a flat paddle. (see

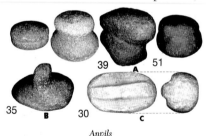

Anvils

Paddle, Wood, and Ceramic Vessel Making Tools).

Anvils were made from about any kind of stone, and, while most are round, some few are rectangular or square. The two outside surfaces on the ends are smooth, and usually slightly convex. The peripheral edge contains a full groove, for ease in handling. Round anvils measure approximately from 1-5/32 to 2½ inches (2.7 to 6.3 cm) high by 2 to 3¾ inches (5.1 to 9.5 cm) in diameter.

The vesicular basalt anvil with the offset rectangular "heads" (A) measures 3 inches (7.6 cm) high with heads 2½ by 3-3/16 inches (6.3 by 8.1 cm).

One of the more peculiar-shaped anvils is (B). This piece was made from vesicular basalt, and has an almost flat 3⅝ by 4⅝ inches (9.2 by 11.7 cm) work surface. It has a projecting 1½ inches (3.8 cm) long oval-shaped hand grip. The entire piece was abraded quite smooth.

The indurated limestone anvil (C), which slightly resembles a kind of shaft straightener, is another odd-shaped anvil. The rough surfaces left when the piece was shaped and a total lack of an abraded or polished finish on any part, beside the shape, make it different. The anvil contains an 11/16 inch (1.74 cm) wide ridge, which extends the length of the piece, measuring 3¾ inches (9.52 cm) long by 2-3/16 inches (5.55 cm) wide.

Apache Tear: These are small irregular-shaped unworked black obsidian nodules of volcanic glass. They are sometimes miscalled "obsidianites." "Beds" of this material are found scattered throughout areas of the Southwest. (refer to "Ceremonial Object").

Apache Tears

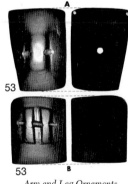

Arm and Leg Ornaments

Arm and Leg Ornament: These ornaments of personal adornment were made from jet, a kind of lignite. They were abraded smooth on the obverse side, while the reverse side was worked to contain attaching loops similar to those found on buttons (see Button). The pair were recovered from a burial located to the north of Roosevelt Lake, Arizona. The larger ornament (A) measures 3-19/32 by 2-9/16 to 2-1/16 inches (9.02 by 6.51 to 5.23 cm) and was found next to the middle of the left fibula/tibia (leg) bones. The smaller piece (B) measures 2-15/16 by 2½ inches (7.47 by 6.35 cm) and was next to the middle of the left humerus (arm) bone. They were obviously worn on the leg and arm as found. The three spots (white in the picture) on the obverse side of (A) are actually turquoise inlay pieces in the jet. The loops on the reverse sides were used to secure the ornaments to the parts of the appendages noted.

Armlet, see Bracelet

Arrow: Actually, an arrow was a heavier and longer version of the combined main shaft and foreshaft of the atlatl dart. The main shaft of an arrow was usually made from a hollow reed, and the foreshaft of a hard wood. These were spliced, generally with animal gut or cactus fibers, which, when dry, would firmly secure the splice together. Arrows usually contained three feathers at one end, secured equi-spaced and parallel to the shaft. The feathers aid the arrow to a straight flight. The arrowpoint was secured to the other end. However, more arrows

39

Spliced Main and Foreshaft of Arrows

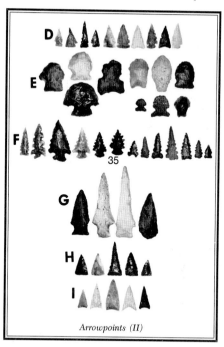

Arrowpoints (II)

were found with the hardwood ends pointed than were found with attached stone points. Many arrow shafts were decorated with bands of various colors, or even simple geometrics. These are said to indicate certain arrows for specific purposes (Peckham, 1965.6-8 and Fig. 4).

Arrowpoint: Arrowpoints are sometimes called "**projectile points.**" There is some discrepancy as to the length a projectile point must be to be classified as a spearpoint. The making of each and the materials from which they were made are similar, based generally upon the local hard or tough stone available. Probably the most common materials used were flint, petrified wood, agate, chert, jasper, basalt, and obsidian. Most arrowpoints were chipped or control-flaked to remove small fragments to the desired size and shape.

Those pictured are a representative group of sizes, shapes, and kinds from different areas of the Southwest. No effort has been made to show completeness of types. It is suggested that for a more detailed or extensive study, the references indicated at the end of this Diction-ary be consulted.

The small points (A) (sometimes called "**bird points**") were usually made from small flakes of obsidian, though other stone was also used.

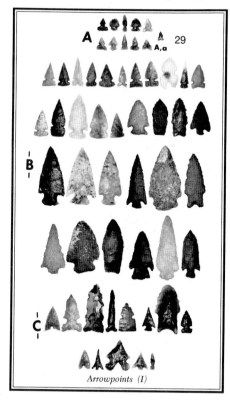

Arrowpoints (I)

Atlatl : Atlatl Weight

One of the smaller obsidian points recovered is (A,a). It measures 5/16 inch (0.79 cm) long. The points in group (B) are a general cross-section of sizes, shapes, and materials from which made. The group (C) is a collection of odd shapes. Undoubtedly each had its own special purpose. (D) pictures a series of "side notched" and "corner notched" points. Note the points were notched on one or both edges or corners with one or a series of as many as four notches on a side. The series (E) are called "stunners," and supposedly were designed to injure, but not kill. The group (F) is a fine collection of serrated points each made from a diferent kind of stone. The points (G) are unique in that each contains a bevel along the right-hand edge as one looks at each side. Such shaping would tend to give the arrow a spiral turning, or "rifled" spin effect when shot from a bow, to deliver greater accuracy. (H and I) are similar, with the exception of the base. (H) points have straight bases, and (I) bases are concaved. It is said that these points were inserted in slits in a wood club, and used much as a mace.

Atlatl: This propellant (sometimes called a "spear thrower," "dart thrower," "throwing stick," or "spear sling") was actually a weapon which enabled the prehistoric Indian to throw a spear or dart harder and farther than a hand-thrown spear. The atlatl adds greater length,

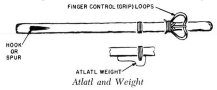

Atlatl and Weight

and so, greater propulsion in throwing a spear or dart.

The piece was a long wood shaft with a finger-grip consisting of two loops at one end, and a hook or spur at the other to hold the base of the spear or dart. When used, the spear lies on top of the atlatl shaft, with the butt end of the spear against the spur. To use this weapon, the arm was drawn back over the shoulder, and whipped forward in a throwing motion, to propel the spear forward, with the fingers in the loops guiding the direction of the spear throw (Peckham, 1965.3-6 and Fig. 1; and Lindsay, *et al*, 1968.64-65).

Atlatl Dart: While the full length of an atlatl shaft is not known, the use and construction of the dart, which, with the shaft, is actually a

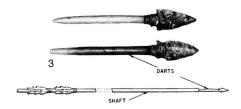

Shaft and Darts for Atlatl

compound weapon, is established (Lindsay, *et al*, 1968.65-67). The main shaft of the projectile was made from hard wood, and was a separate phase of the dart. Because of this, the shaft proper was a reusable feature of the weapon. This part contained the feathered end which guided the missile, and the other end contained a hollow socket in which one end of the dart foreshaft was fitted. A damaged dart could easily be replaced, but obviously, the main shaft was in a different category. A chipped stone point was attached to the dart.

Atlatl Dart Bunt: The dart bunt, a part of the atlatl equipment, was used more as a "stunner" than as a weapon meant to kill (Lindsay, *et al*, 1968. Fig. 42 and p. 67). This piece was a stubby

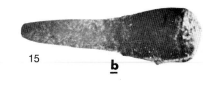

Atlatl Dart Bunt

foreshaft made to be inserted into the end of the shaft. The end, instead of containing a stone projectile point, was padded and bound with animal hide, and sewn securely in place.

Atlatl Weight: Although these stone pieces are presently called a **"weight,"** or **"spear-thrower weight,"** there is some doubt as to whether they actually served the purpose of a weight or a "balance" feature, or were in the nature of a charm to aid the user of the atlatl during the hunt or war.

The weights were well made and abraded smooth, and some even decorated with encircling painted bands, or graved grooves.

Many were perforated to aid in securing the piece to the atlatl. The weight was usually located just forward of the two finger control (grip) loops (see Atlatl illustration).

Awl: Awls were pointed tools used for making holes for sewing skins, weaving, basketry, or other similar uses. These tools should not be confused with needles, punches, drills, and so on. Bone awls enjoyed an almost unlimited use by the prehistoric Indian.

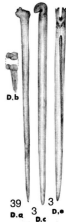

The workmanship found on these tools ranges from crude bone splinters, unworked from the original fortuitous form except for pointing — to beautifully rounded, tapered, and polished shafts with carved joint ends.

39 **A**
Bone Awl

Awls were worked from split cannon bones (between knee and fetlock) of deer, sheep, and antelope; the ulnae (bone in forelimb) of deer containing varying degrees of modification to the articulating head ("A" pictures an awl with an unworked head); tibia (bone of lower leg);

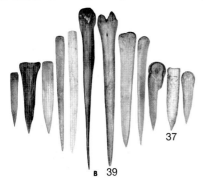

37

B **39**

Bone Awls (Segments)

and other kinds or fragments of bone too numerous to mention (some are shown in the figure [B]).

Awls measure generally from 2-9/32 to 9-13/16 inches (5.8 to 24.9 cm) long. Between these extremes are those awls with the joint left intact at one end (probably as a handhold), and those with joints removed, or partially removed, and the butt ends rounded.

Some awls were perforated at the butt end, or graved with an encircling groove for wearing on a suspension cord for quick use (C,a). Note that awl (C,b) not only contains a perforation at the butt end, but also has been colored with a black matte paint for a

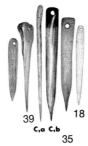

39 **18**
C,a C,b
35

Perforated and Grooved Awls

length of ⅞ inch (2.22 cm) at the same end. The awl had been highly polished.

Bone
Carved Joint End: The carved joint ends of awls pictured (D) include an animal (D,a) and a bird (damaged) (D,b), a sheep horn (D,c) and antelope horn (D,d). They were carved with stone knives and worked by abrasion. Such life forms are not considered charms, *per se*, but merely ornamentation added to the tool at the whim of the awl maker. These are fairly scarce.

D.b

Spatulate End: Many bone awl-like implements which contain spatulate ends have been found. It is believed that these were hair ornaments, which were probably worn by both men and women (see Hair Ornament).

39 **3**
D.a **3** **D,e**
D.c

Awls, Carved Joint Ends

Specialized: These so-called "specialized" awls are those containing special shaped points or shafts (E). Instead of the regular tapering points, these are bodkin, full cylindrical, needle, etc. All were obviously made for some special use.

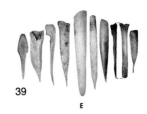

39

E

Specialized Awls

Wood
The two wood awls pictured were made from splinters of wood, and were recovered by excavation. The points are well made and tapered, though the shafts are unworked. Generally, awls made from wood were recovered from dry caves, and not by excavation.

Awl Pointer: These implements were made from coarse to fine grades of abrasive stone such as sandstone, rhyolite, vesicular basalt, and many other kinds of local abrasive stone. While many were pecked

Wood Awls

Axe

into oval, rectangular, square, or odd shapes (A), some were also made from unshaped chunks, or from waterworn pieces of granite, basalt, and other stone (B). They are usually differentiated from shaft abraders or smoothers by having a considerably thinner groove(s), which was

30

A

Awl Pointer

used for the pointing of bone awls, wood foreshafts of atlatls and arrows, stone points, and so on.

In addition to active, or hand-held awl pointers, large slabs of sandstone and other fine abrasive tabular stone were used for pointing, or re-pointing awls (C). The large irregular-shaped tan sandstone slab pictured had recived a considerable amount of usage, as shown

56 **B**

39 **C**
i2"=1'-0"=30.5 CM.

56 **B**

Awl Pointers

by the "markings" on the piece. The slab measures, roughly, 13 by 18 inches (33.0 by 46.7 cm).

Axe: Axes (sometimes called "**celt**," and often called "**tomahawks**") were made from almost any hard stone, and were notched in several different ways for hafting. The piece pictured

38

Axe Handle

is an axe handle made from a section of a yucca flower stem. The loop contained an axe, which was missing when the handle was found. The cord which had secured the handle to the axe groove was made from yucca fibers. The piece came from a cave near Camp Verde in Arizona.

These tools and weapons first appeared during the later Basketmaker III (A.D. 500-750)

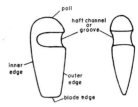

poll

haft channel or groove

inner edge

outer edge

blade edge

Axe Nomenclature

period. The nomenclature of the parts of axes is given in the Figure. Most axes were pecked to general shape, then abraded to varying degrees of smoothness, and sometimes even polished. The groove or haft channel of the axe was usually the only part not polished, though some were slightly abraded. This was to permit the hafting a better grip.

Some axes were shaped by chipping and all have sharpened blade edges (A). The sharpened blade edge makes the tool or weapon a very effective piece. Some also show evidence of pecking and abrading of the piece. These axes are said to be of an earlier make than those only pecked and abraded to shape. This is also indicated by the irregular shaping, as opposed to the balanced shapes and polish of later axes.

Some axes were rough-shaped by pecking (B), showing both three-quarter and full grooves, and with flat and rounded polls. There is no other evidence of further work on these axes. They were neither abraded nor polished, nor even chipped. It is suggested that work on these axes was interrupted for some reason, thus they were never finished or used.

Other axes were made from flattish, elongated waterworn stones which could be further pecked to shape with a minimum amount of effort (C). Such axes were generally grooved on each side edge for hafting.

Blade lengths and widths vary, as do the flat to rounded polls. Axes generally measure from 2¼ to 8¾ inches (5.9 to 22.3 cm) long, and weigh from 0.37 to 4.19 lbs. In general, axes are found in many variations of the shapes, kinds, and sizes pictured.

The pointed tip axe (D) is similar to others, with the exception that the poll is flat, and the working end is pointed, instead of bladed. This tool was undoubtedly a utility implement, and was probably used to reduce stone (paint pigment) for later grinding. Note that there is only a general uniformity of axes.

The following breakdown is presented in an effort to familiarize the student with the general points of differentiation.

Axes which were edge grooved are similar to others, with the exception that the two extreme edges only were pecked for hafting.

The full grooved axe (E) is probably the more typical of the hafting utilization. These

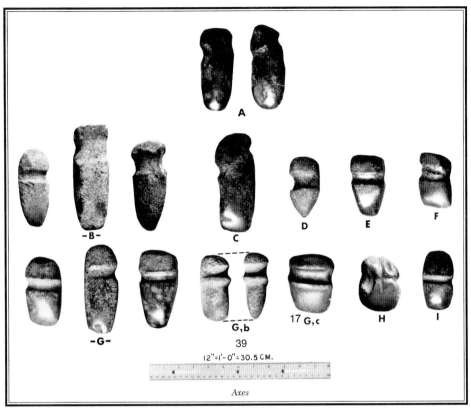

Axes

were pecked to a complete encircling groove for the hafting.

The unique spiral groove (F) permits the hafting to encircle the axe a full one and three-quarter turns. The double groove was set at a slight diagonal to the longitudinal axis of the axe. This type of hafting is probably the most scarce of those indicated herein.

Three-quarter grooved axes (G) are similar to most others, with the exception that the groove for hafting was pecked only three-quarters around the periphery of the axe. The part not grooved was usually located on the inside edge, as the axe was hafted. One of the longest three-quarter grooved axes (G,a) measures 8⅝ inches (21.91 cm) long. It is one of the better made and

Axes

balanced axes found. It was recovered by excavation near Prescott, Arizona.

Some of these three-quarter grooved axes contain a flare immediately below and parallel to the groove (G,b, side and front views shown), while some contain a flare both below and above the groove (G,c).

Note that the double flared axe (G,d) contains two features which are different from other axes. There is a thin transverse groove below the lower flare which accentuates the flare. Additionally, this axe contains a vertical groove extending above and below the rear of the lower flare. It is assumed that this groove was used to insert a wedge between the rear of the axe (hafting area) and the lashings to better secure the handle in place.

Axes with a kind of cross-grooving for hafting (H) are quite scarce. The axe pictured, made from a chunk of gray basalt, was recovered from a small pueblo ruin west of Los Lunas, New Mexico. The piece was chipped and pecked to shape, then abraded. The full transverse groove encircles the

27

piece, and an additional groove, extending from below the transverse groove on both flat sides, extends up and over the rough-shaped poll.

Those thought to be war axes (I) were generally smaller than most double bitted axes, and sometimes even better made than those for utility purposes. They were pecked to shape and highly polished. Many of these were made from more colorful stone, and so were highly prized. A double bitted axe is very similar to modern axes of the same type. Such axes as the pointed kind (D) are sometimes also classified as "war" axes.

Axes which have had the blade edge resharpened may be readily determined (J),

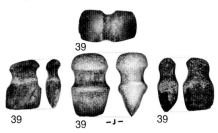

Axes

because the blade is generally shorter, and usually contains an angle, or bevel, of rework. Such blades were reworked when they became chipped, partially dulled, or completely dulled.

The two zoomorphic marked axes (K) were recovered from a Hohokam ruin located to the south of Phoenix, Arizona. The axe (K,a) made from basalt, contains an assumed simulated reptile, which was pecked in bas-relief into the outer or leading edge of the axe. This axe is three-quarter grooved (see, G). It measures 6⅞ inches (17.46 cm) long, and weighs 2.44 lbs. Axe (K,b) was made from granite, and contains a bird also pecked in bas-relief. The entire axe (K,b), except the groove and blade edge, has been pecked to simulate a bird. Detail includes the beak, head, eyes, crest, wings (feathers), tail, and legs. The axe was originally full grooved (see, E). It measures 6-11/16 inches (16.9 cm) long, and weighs 1.9 lbs. The elaboration of

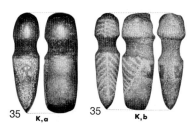

Decorated Axes

the bird and reptile pecked into these axes is not of a ceremonial nature, but undoubtedly was worked at the whim of the makers of the axes.

While the re-use of an axe as a hammerstone might be considered the "downgrading" of a previously specialized tool, it also indicates a degree of thrift, because of the continued use of the implement. When an axe blade edge became damaged, or even worn beyond the point of re-sharpening, these axes became hand-held hammerstones, or pounders (see Hammerstone).

Axe Sharpener: The implements pictured were made from large rectangular chunks of vesic-cular basalt or other abrasive stone. These were pecked and abraded to shape. The implements are identified by one or more wide length-wise depressions or grooves, worn by the repeated sharpening or resharpening of axe blades (Martin, 1961.96 and Fig. 69).

Such tools measure approximately

Axe Sharpeners

10½ inches (26.7 cm) long by 5 inches (12.7 cm) wide by 3½ inches (8.9 cm) thick, and weigh up to 8 to 9 lbs. Note that axe sharpener (A) was used from both ends, as indicated by the slightly angled groove starting at each end. (B) only contains a single groove for its entire length.

Ball, Game, see Ball, Stone

Ball, Pitch: Balls of this sort were formed by large blobs of resin which was taken from certain evergreen trees (*pinus edulis*), and applied with a yucca fiber brush. The pitch material was heated to the consistency of thick molasses. A heavy brush of

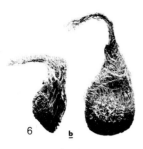

Pitch Pall

yucca fibers was dipped into the heated pitch, then smeared as evenly as possible over the woven basket, canteen, or whatever receptacle was being waterproofed. The process is sometimes called "caulking." The heated pitch was also smeared on the inside surface of the container to aid in the waterproofing action. During the process of covering the container, the pitch hardened somewhat. A final action consisted of revolving the container slowly over the fire to give a more smooth or even coverage of the pitch on the exterior surface. The remaining blob of pitch which accumulated on the heavy yucca fiber brush accounts for the nomenclature given the brush.

Ball, Rubber: Such balls, presumedly used on the ball courts of the Southwest, are thought to be an importation from the south (Mexico). This presupposes a knowledge of a substance containing the resilient properties of rubber was found in "*guayule*," a plant found in the area of present day Chihuahua, Mexico. A rubber ball was found in a Hohokam site of the Sedentary Period located near Toltec, Arizona. The maximum diameter of this ball is 3-13/16 inches (8.6 cm) (Gladwin and Haury, 1965.48).

It is supposed that the religious and social life centered around ball courts. The ball game played could have been a variation of a Mayan game played by two teams using a solid rubber ball. (One such ball was found near Gila Bend, Arizona [Colton, 1960.65]). Other Hohokam villages contained similar ball courts (Gladwin and Haury, 1965.36-49). Not only have such ball courts been found in the Hohokam sites in the area of Phoenix, Arizona (see Map in Prehistoric Cultural Periods section), but six known courts have been found in Hohokam sites in the vicinity of the San Francisco Peaks, which were built subsequent to the arrival in the area of the Hohokam Indians in A.D. 1065 (Colton,

1960.44-45, 49, 65). Archaeological evidence indicates that the old game(s) for which ball courts were originally used was abandoned about A.D. 1400 (Gladwin and Haury, 1965.49).

Ball, Stone: Stone balls (sometimes called "**stone spheres**" or "**game balls**") are not to be confused with worn-out hammerstones. Stone balls have been pecked spherical and smoothed intentionally, and exhibit no evidence of either flat

Stone Balls

(facet) or rough surfaces. They were made from agate, granite, chert, and other stone of this nature. They range from 2 to 3½ inches (5.1 to 8.8 cm) in diameter.

These balls are said to have been used in a game involving rolling of the ball into a distant hole. Another game in which balls were used was "*tejo*." This game is said to have been adopted by the Spanish colonists from the prehistoric Indians. The action involves the pitching of the ball high into the air, and attempting to drop the piece into a hole twice the diameter of the stone, and approximately 50 feet (15.24 meters) away.

It is also thought that such balls might have been used as maces, or even in a sling.

It is quite possible that the smaller smooth balls might have been used as grinding stones in small rectangular mortars (see Mortar). The stones would have been rolled by hand in a rotary motion to crush small seeds, or to pulverize small amounts of stone pigment.

Baton: These are staffs which are symbols of authority (sometimes called "**scepters**"). They were undoubtedly carried by a religious functionary, or some other official concerned with the leadership of a ceremonial nature. Whatever the purpose of the baton, it was not of a utilitarian nature. Items of this kind have been recovered which were made from stone and wood.

Stone: The stone baton (A) is an elliptically-shaped purple quartz piece. It measures 2-3/16 inches (5.5 cm) major axis in transverse section by 15 inches (38.1 cm) long. From the

Batten

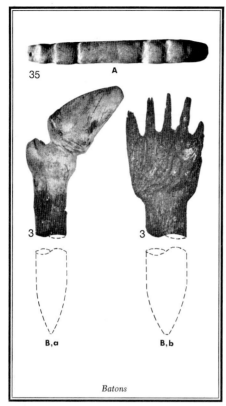

Batons

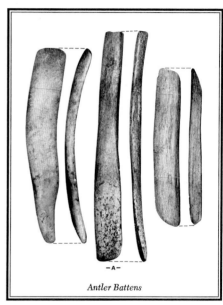

Antler Battens

while the weft was inserted, and to beat the weft down into place. They were used with a vertical loom.

Antler: Battens of this kind were made from tines which had been split in half lengthwise. The inside was abraded smooth, and the ends rounded and slightly beveled. These implements are said to have been used in the making of twilled matting, baskets, and other weaving operations.

Bone: These battens were made from mammal bone. Batten (A) was recovered at Tonque Pueblo (Barnett, 1969.103). It is a

Bone Battens

rounded shaft measuring 10¾ inches (27.3 cm) long, and is blunt-pointed at each end. The piece was made from a length of large mammal leg bone.

The second batten (B) was recovered from a ruin north of Quemado, New Mexico. This implement, also made from a segment of a mammal leg bone, was not as well smoothed as batten (A), though the rough edges of the bone have been slightly abraded. The ends were rounded, and one contains a slightly blunted chisel-like edge. The piece measures 7⅝ inches (19.2 cm) long.

middle, and extending at measured intervals toward each end, are a series of equi-spaced encircling grooves. A hole was started on the flange at each end, one on one side and one on the other. The baton was recovered from Tonque Pueblo (Barnett, 1969.116).

Wood: Two rounded sticks, pointed at one end and containing carved symbols at the other, were recovered from a cave north of Flagstaff, Arizona.

The first staff (B,a) contains a well shaped deer hoof carved at one end of the 14½ inch (36.83 cm) long piece. The hoof and hock were painted blue, and the staff was well rounded.

The second staff (B,b) is a rather crude carving of a human hand. The piece is 20 inches (50.8 cm) long. It cannot be determined if the piece was painted or not as the entire piece is charred.

Batten: Battens, made from mammal bone, antler, and probably wood, were used during weaving operations to keep warp sets apart

Bead: These items of personal adornment were the most prevalent decoration worn by the prehistoric Indian. Materials such as shell, stone, bone, and clay material were commonly used. Of these, stone enjoyed the widest coverage. Stone of both a decorative or a semi-precious gem nature, as well as shale, slate, and other ordinary tabular stone was used.

Many small pendants (actually "drops") are often considered as beads. Generally, pendants are perforated at one end or side with one or more holes, while a bead is usually perforated near the center with a single hole for stringing.

Beads of any kind, involving the use of local materials, were used for personal adornment almost from the beginning of time. Beads made from shell and other materials are first recorded as having been worn in the Southwest by the Basketmaker II people (A.D. 1 to 450-500).

Clay: Clay beads are considered quite scarce. These generally spherically-shaped beads range from ½ to 1-1/16 inches (1.27 to 2.80 cm) in diameter, and contain a small single hole through the center. Some of these beads contain traces of a brown-red matte paint (probably hematite).

Of the four spherical clay beads shown (A), two were recovered at Tonque Pueblo (Barnett, 1969.30, 99); one north of Quemado, New Mexico; and one from Fitzmaurice Pueblo (Barnett, 1973).

The odd dumbbell-shaped clay bead (A,a) was found to the east of Phoenix, Arizona, near a small ruin. A bead of this shape is considered a rarity.

Holes in clay beads were made by forcing a twig through the center while the clay material was still wet and pliable. When the piece was fired, the twig would burn out, leaving the hole.

Conus Shell: In addition to use as a "tinkler" (see Pendant [Shell, C,b]), conus shells were also strung in necklaces. The apex of the spire was abraded off, leaving a small hole (B). A cord was strung through the hole and out the canal end.

Discoidal Bone: Discoidal bone beads were made from thin bits of bone material, generally sliced from a larger tubular mammal bone. Such beads are shaped round, and perforated with a single hole. They are abraded smooth on both sides and on the peripheral edge.

While bead (C) is not of discoidal bone, it was made from an allied material, horn. It is almost cylindrical, and considering the material, is a scarcity. The horn bead pictured was

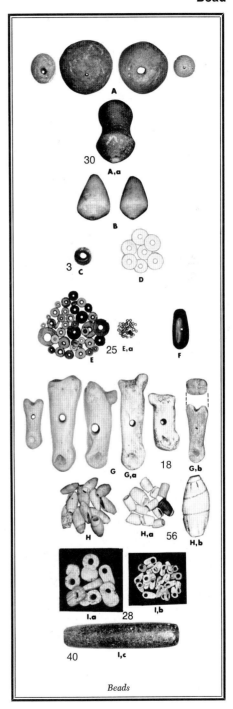

Beads

recovered from a cave in Northeastern Arizona.

Discoidal Shell: These beads (D) were made from larger valves of bivalve shells. Various diameter discs were cut from the shell, and the pieces then drilled. The periphery was abraded, and both exterior surfaces then abraded flat.

Discoidal Stone: Discoidal stone beads of various diameters and thickness (E) were made from turquoise, argillite, slate, gypsum, shale, limestone, and many other ornamental and semi-precious gem stones (see Color Plate I, Item 4, p. 10. The flat surfaces and periphery were abraded quite smooth. The sequence of discoidal bead making is shown in Color Plate I, Item 5, p. 10. (The pump drill shown is similar to those used by the prehistoric Indian).

Among the smallest discoidal stone beads recovered are those made from a black slate (E,a). Those pictured are of the same scale as other beads pictured in the general bead grouping.

Jet: Beads made from jet (a lignite material) were sometimes discoidal, or other odd shapes. The one pictured (F) was ellipsoidal, and was perforated through the middle. The piece exhibits a high polish.

Mammal Metatarsal Bone: Such beads (G) were made from large mammal metatarsal bones. The piece was drilled through near the center of the shaft for stringing transversely in a necklace. The joint ends of many were carved with an animal head (G,a), while others were carved with a deep "+" in one end (G,b). Most of the bones were polished. Those pictured were recovered by excavation north of Quemado, New Mexico.

Olivella Shell: Of the various kinds of shells worked for stringing in a necklace, the most popular was the olivella shell (H). Most of these shells merely had the apex of the spire abraded off, which produced a hole for stringing. However, many were also abraded on the canal end, which gave the shell a cylindrical appearance (H,a). A few of the shells were graved, additionally, with spirals or simple geometrics for elaboration (H,b, enlarged).

Tubular Bone: Based upon diameters of ⅛ to 9/16 inch (0.25 to 1.4 cm), and sections cut ⅜ to 4¾ inches (1.0 to 12.1 cm) long, these beads were sometimes called **"plain tubes"** (see "Tubular Bone" picture). They were made from small to large tubular bones from rodents and large birds. The joint ends were

removed, and the remaining shaft was then cut into lengths as desired. Most tubular bead ends were abraded smooth, and the shaft sometimes polished.

Tubular beads were strung end-to-end in a necklace, though some were drilled through

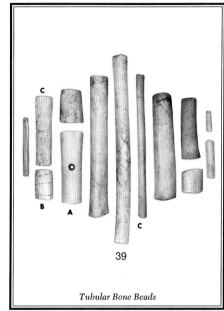

39

Tubular Bone Beads

the middle of the tube length (A), and could also be strung transversely. Many of the tubular beads were graved throughout their length with spirals or simple geometrics (B), while others contain one or more light encircling grooves (C).

Miscellaneous Odd Shapes: These are flat limestone beads of other than discoidal shape. There are many variations of these found throughout the Southwest. The larger limestone beads (I,a) were shaped similar to a figure "8" or a "keyhole." While the smaller versions (I,b) are similar, they are more generally ellipsoidal in shape.

The 2⅜ inches (6.0 cm) long cylindrical bead (I,c) was made from a piece of basalt. The bead contains a slight taper toward each end, which was rounded. The piece was highly polished.

Bead Polishing Stone, see Abrading Slab

Beaming Knife, see Flesher

Beaming Tool, see Flesher

Beam Support, see Floor-Beam Support

Beating Stick, see Seed Beater

Bell: One of the unique rarities made by the prehistoric Indian was his bells. These were made from both clay and copper. Because of the loops on copper bells, and the one or two holes in the clay bells, it is concluded that these items were worn in a necklace, or on arm- or leg-bands. Considering their comparative scarcity, it is assumed that bells were worn during ceremonial dances or on other ceremonial occasions. However, it might be noted that the sound emitted by a single bell is actually a very

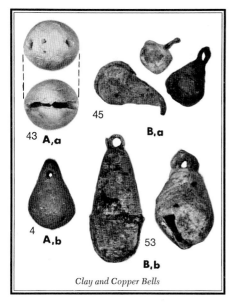

43 **A,a** 45

4 **A,b** 53

B,a

B,b

Clay and Copper Bells

light "tinkling" sound. Thus, it would take many of these bells to develop sufficient volume of sound which could be readily heard. For this reason, such bells were undoubtedly more of a decorative feature than musical.

Clay: Some clay bells (A,a, top and bottom views shown) are smooth and almost spherical in shape. They contain a 1/16 to 3/32 inch (0.16 to 0.24 cm) wide slit in the bottom which extends approximately half way around the piece. There are two 3/32 inch diameter (0.24 cm) holes in the back for attaching the piece. The inside contains a small ball clapper, also made from clay. The bell was fired, and is a light tan color containing several small smoke clouds. The clay bell (A,a) was recovered from a dry cave located along the

Verde River to the west of Camp Verde, Arizona.

The clay bell (A,b), which is pear-shaped, contains a single hole at the top for attaching. There is a slit at the bottom, and a small clay ball clapper is contained within the bell. The bell is one inch (2.54 cm) high.

Copper: Copper bells (B,a) (sometimes called "**resonators**") are usually pear-shaped, and contain a small loop at the tapered top for wearing. They contain a narrow slit at the bottom, and either a small stone pebble or copper pellet as a clapper. Bells of this kind were made by a casting method, and have been recovered from several prehistoric pueblo ruins in the Southwest (Gladwin, Haury, Sayles, and Gladwin, 1965.163-165, 278-281).

The two copper bells (B,b) are considerably larger than those pictured immediately above. Note, also, that the shell of the large copper bell on the left was made in two sections. Both large bells contain a loop at the top for wearing. The slits at the bottom of these bells are considerably larger than those in bells (B,a).

Bell Stone, see Chime

Bin Cover: These covers were large, though comparatively thin, slabs of tabular sandstone,

12"×1'-0"×30.5 CM.

Bin Covers

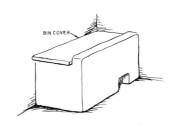

BIN COVER

Use of Bin Cover

Bird Call : Bracelet

rhyolite, limestone, slate, or other local tabular stone. They were usually chipped into a rectangular shape and sized to fit as a cover over storage bins built into corners of pueblo-type rooms. Covers generally measure from ⅜ to ¾ inch (0.9 to 1.9 cm) thick.

Bird Call: This crude instrument was made from two sherds whose concave sides face each other and were bound together with twisted yucca fibers. The sherds were shaped generally round by chipping, but are not matching. The sherd edges were rough chipped. The two sherd pieces are slightly convex, and probably held a blade of grass or a thin reed when used. The edge of the piece was blown into as a wind instrument.

4

Bird Call

Bird Point, see Arrowpoint (A)

Boiling Stone, see Cooking Stone

Bow: Bows and arrows came into being in the Southwest during the mid-14th Century and are a rarity. Some fragments have been found in dry caves, but only a very few whole bows. The "self-bow," *i.e.,* a bow made from a single stave of wood, was considered the most common. Generally, bows with an arc, or simple curve, were more in use than double-curved or "cupid's bow" shapes.

Bracelet: A bracelet (sometimes called an "arm-

let") is an ornamental band worn about the wrist, forearm, or even around the upper arm (biceps). Such ornaments were made from shell and stone, though those made of stone are the more rare. The small size bracelets were made for children, and the larger for men or women.
Shell: Various widths were cut from the encircling edge of large valves of bivalve shells (*glycymeris*). This produced bracelets of different sizes and widths, depending upon the diameter of the shell used. Such ornaments were abraded smooth around the edges.

The bracelets (A) are quite thin, and are plain in that they do not contain any graving, inlay, or overlay work. Bracelets (B) were both graved with simple repeated geometric designs. They are both the same diameter, and well graved. (B,a) has the more intricate series of design motifs, and (B,b) is the plainer. The layout of graving on both bracelets illustrates the repeated basic design elements.

Note that on the right-hand side of the bracelet (B,a) there are two sets of small repair holes. Each pair of holes is spaced approximately 5/16 inch (0.79 cm) apart (one hole on each side of the break). These holes were used to repair the bracelet when it became damaged. Usually fresh yucca fibers or gut from small mammals were strung through the holes, and when dried would pull the break tightly together.
Stone: The stone bracelet pictured (C) was made from argillite. It was well rounded, and both inside and outside edges were beveled. It was abraded smooth (note striations on flat surface from abrasive). The only embellishment was the small protruding knob on the

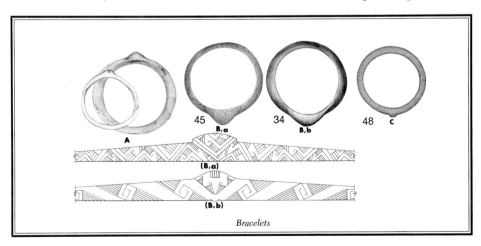

45 **B,a** 34 **B,b** 48 **c**

A

(B,a)

(B,b)

Bracelets

outer edge (maybe made in imitation of a shell).

Breastplate, Bone: The pieces of rib bones each contain a hole drilled near each end. It is not known whether the five polished pieces pictured constituted an entire breastplate or not.

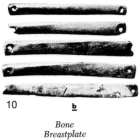

10   **b**

Bone Breastplate

These were recovered in a group, and are assumed to have been the complete plate. A cord was strung through the perforations at the ends, drawing the pieces close together. The cord probably extended up and around the neck, which helped keep the plate in place on the chest. The bone lengths are graduated, measuring from 5¼ to 6½ inches (13.8 to 16.5 cm) long.

Brush, see Hair Brush, Yucca; or Paint Brush

Bull-Roarer: As the name implies, this unique artifact is a noise-maker, and is said to have been a ceremonial piece. The object consists of a large mammal sternum (breastbone) which was wrapped in a piece of well dried-out deer hide, and which was secured with gut. A stick was attached with a length of gut to one end of exposed bone. The piece was used by holding the stick firmly, and swinging the deer-hide covered bone piece rapidly around and around. This motion produced a deep whirring, almost a moaning sound. The item was recovered from a cave south of Phoenix, Arizona.

53

Bull-Roarer

Bundle, Juniper-Bark: These loosely wrapped bundles of unshredded peel of strips of juniper

bark are secured with additional strips. They are thought to have been used as caulking in ceiling construction. These bundles were recovered in Northern Arizona (Judd, 1954. 276-278).

12   **b**

Juniper-Bark Bundles

Burial Slab: Burial slabs of the kind shown were used in funerary rites by many of the prehistoric Indian cultures. In general, the practice was to place the deceased (often flexed) in a hole in the ground. Then after placing offerings or the possessions of the individual around the remains, a slab containing a hole was placed over the body, and the crypt filled with dirt and sometimes large rocks.

It is the opinion of some archaeologists that the hole in the slab was made to permit the escape of the soul or breath body, or even evil

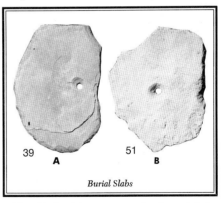

39   **A**   51   **B**

Burial Slabs

spirits. Such slabs were made from tabular sandstone, limestone, granite, or other tabular stone native to the area concerned. Some of the slabs were drilled or reamed, while others were not. Slabs are rectangular, square, round, and various irregular shapes. The edges were usually rough chipped.

The slabs pictured each contain a double countersunk-type (biconical) hole (drilled and/or reamed from both sides). The holes measure ¾ inch (1.9 cm) in diameter. Slab (A) was recovered from Tonque Pueblo Ruin (Barnett, 1969.

35

132) and slab (B) was recovered from a ruin at Middle Verde, Arizona.

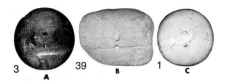

3   39   **B**   1   C

A

Buttons

Button: Most "buttons" are only differentiated from a perforated disc or a pendant by the method of perforation for attaching. In a stone button, the hole does not penetrate through the piece. Regardless of the shape of the button, the reverse side contains a ridge near the center. Two holes were drilled, one from each side of the ridge and at a slight downward angle through the ridge, to meet in the middle.

These pieces were usually made from a com-

paratively soft stone, for ease of abrasion and perforation.

Jet: The jet button (A) (a kind of lignite) is round and measures 29/32 inch (2.2 cm) in diameter. It was well smoothed and polished, and has a rounded edge. The button was recovered from a ruin in Northern Arizona.

Pink Slate: The irregularly-shaped pink slate button (B) was considerably more crudely made than the one of jet (above). Striations from abrasion in evidence on both sides, and the lack of symmetry both indicate little concern for the finished appearance of the piece. This button was recovered from a ruin to the west of Albuquerque, New Mexico.

Shell: The shell button shown (C) measures 2-1/16 inches (5.24 cm) in diameter, and contains two holes for attaching. The convex surface was abraded smooth, as was the reverse, so that the shell is unidentifiable as to variety. The edge was also abraded smooth. (Lindsay, 1968.63 and Fig. 39 d-f).

Celt, see Axe

Ceramic Vessel Making Tools: These implements vary to a small degree from one culture to another. In general, there were two major methods of fabricating ceramic wares. In lieu of a potter's wheel (which none of the cultures had), many potters used parts of broken jars or bowls as a base (called a "pottery form") from which to "start" a new vessel. In making miniatures, a drier consistency of clay was used and the vessel shaped by hand.

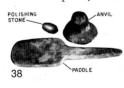

38

Ceramic Vessel Making Tools

The "paddle and anvil" method was used to flatten out the clay rope coils. This consisted of winding the coils of clay to the approximate contour desired for the finished piece. The implements pictured include a 12-7/16 inches (31.59 cm) long wood paddle, a mushroom-shaped anvil, and a waterworn polishing stone. All were recovered together in a cave along the Verde River, near Camp Verde, Arizona. The anvil (see Anvil) was held against the inside wall while the surface was patted smooth with a wooden paddle (see Paddle, Wood).

After the vessel was dry, a polishing stone (see Polishing Stone) was used with water for the final dressing of the outer surface. The more the polishing stone was used, the higher the polish.

In the second method, only a smoothing implement (see Pottery Smoothing Implement) was used to dress off excess clay from both the inside and outside surfaces. In this method, the paddle and anvil were not used. However, a polishing stone was undoubtedly employed to give a final smoothness to the outer surface.

Ceremonial Axe: Ceremonial axes (or pounders) are actually not "axes" *per se,* but are suggested as ceremonial or symbolic, because the light material from which most of them were made is too soft for any utility usage. They were generally rough-shaped by chipping, much in the form of a modern double-bitted axe. Each were edge-grooved near the center by chipping, indicating that they were probably hafted. Other than the rough-shape (and except for [C]) there was no effort to abrade the blade, or to sharpen the blade edge.

Those pictured were shaped by chipping from white or silver quartz (A) (which weighs 0.56 oz.), and banded calcite (B) of comparable weight. The axe in the middle of the first three large pieces measures 6¾ inches (17 cm) long

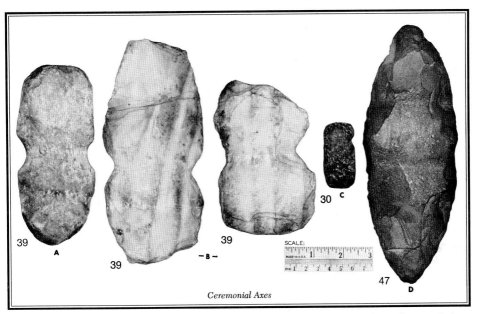

Ceremonial Axes

by ⅝ inch (1.6 cm) thick. They were recovered by excavation from the Tonque Pueblo Ruins (Barnett, 1969.108).

The miniature axe (C), which measures 2-3/16 inches (5.5 cm) long, is three-quarter grooved, and pecked to shape, then abraded. It is possible that this small axe was made for a child, but more probably it was either used ceremonially, or even as a weapon.

The large boat-shaped axe (D) was crudely chipped to shape from a slab of basalt. Each end was round pointed. The edges were chipped to a general sharpness. Each edge contains an edge-groove for hafting. The entire surface of both sides, with the exception of the side areas between the edge grooves, was painted with a brown-red color (probably hematite). Because of the colored blades, the piece is considered as ceremonial, and because of the edge grooves is classified as an axe (see Chipped and Notched Tool).

Ceremonial Disc, Painted:

These discs were well made from tabular sandstone. They were smoothed on both sides, and have rounded edges. (Such pieces illustrate the close

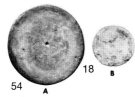

Painted Ceremonial Discs

approach to a wheel by the prehistoric Indians of the Southwest, without their actually using a wheel, as such, to turn on a central axis.)

The 11½ inches (29.2 cm) diameter disc (A) with the partially drilled center, was made from a one inch (2.5 cm) thick piece of tabular sandstone which had been abraded smooth, and which contains a rounded edge. The piece was painted with a green center and a heavy concentric white circle, with an encircling red band which extends over the rounded periphery. The piece was recovered from a ruin along the Rio Puerco, west of Albuquerque, New Mexico.

The smaller disc (B) measures 6 inches (15.24 cm) in diameter. The outer periphery was painted dark green, and the large center painted yellow. A painted black line separated the two colors.

Because of the colors and configuration, these discs are assumed to have been used during a ceremony by the prehistoric Indians.

Ceremonial Object:

These are items of material culture, usually of a custom or religious significance, to which feeling and action are directed. Such items may have been used, not only in the rituals or practices of the medicine men, but of other individuals as well.

The extent of bona fide ceremonial objects is practically unlimited, for many might be considered for other purposes. For example, many

37

Details of Unusual Ceremonial Objects

musical instruments fall into this category, as they were probably used for social as well as ritual expression. For this reason, only those items readily identifiable as "ceremonial" are included as such. Those artifacts which are merely "suspect" (because of lack of positive identification or obscurity) are not included as objects with a ceremonial use or purpose.

Objects of a ceremonial nature are made from bone, clay material, potsherds, shell, and stone. Most of these were well made, though generally symbolic. However, some were quite crudely fashioned, and especially those hand-molded from various clay materials.

The objects pictured are grouped according to material, and illustrate the variety of such items used by the prehistoric Indians.

The following listing of ceremonial objects is included as a guide to the ceremonial artifacts included in this Dictionary:

Apache Tear	Medicine Box
Baton	Medicine Tube
Bell	Paho, Turkey
Bull-Roarer	Feather
Burial Slab	Painted Shell
Ceremonial Axe	Painted Stone
Ceremonial Disc,	Pipe
Painted	Plaque
Chime	Prayer Stick
Crystal	Pricklypear Cactus
Cylinder, Ves. Bas.	Fruit,
Small	Reproduction of
Disc,	Sipapu
Multiperforated	Smoking Tube
Fetish	Statue, Effigy
Figurine, Human	Tinkler, Bone
Flower, Wood	Trumpet
Flute	Whistle
Guiro	Whistle, Bitsitsi
Koshare Symbol	Yucca Seed Pod,
Lightning Stone	Reproduction of
Mammal Scapulae,	
Decorated	

Details of Unusual Ceremonial Objects: The following descriptive material includes details of some of the more unusual or specialized ceremonial objects, *i.e.*, these in addition to those items listed above. Some of the objects are pictured in two or three views. This permits a more detailed study of the configuration and markings (whether by carving, abrasion, or painting) of the piece.

The frog (A) is a polychrome clay piece which measures 4-3/16 inches (10.6 cm) long. This item is one of the more accurate replicas which has been recovered. The piece was painted with black stripes and dots on a tan base color on the back, sides, and head. The underbelly is a brown-red color. An oddity of the piece pictured is the open mouth.

The double-knob and cylindrical bar-shaped basalt (B,a), while quite different, seems (by the very kind of item) to be a ceremonial piece, possibly of the phallus involving a maturation rite. The piece, which was abraded quite smooth, measures 4⅝ inches (11.8 cm) long by 1-9/32 inches (3.25 cm) diameter near the middle. A hole was drilled through just below the upper knob. An item quite similar in appearance to that pictured was recovered just to the west of the Arizona border (Miles, 1968.156-157).

Object (B,b) is of the nature of a mature phallus. It was made cylindrical from orange-colored sandstone, and was abraded quite smooth. This piece was also undoubtedly used during a ceremonial maturation rite similar to item (B,a). It

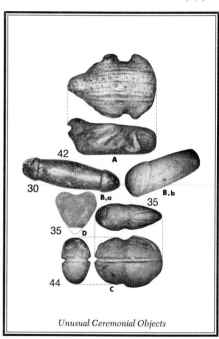

Unusual Ceremonial Objects

measures 6 inches (15.24 cm) long by 1¾ inches (4.44 cm) in diameter. The "head" is slightly larger. A fine groove encircles the piece at the end opposite to the "head." The piece was recovered from a ruin north of Quemado, New Mexico.

The stylized animal (C) was carved and abraded from what had originally been a full-grooved (with both edge-grooves pecked) ceremonial axe made from green quartz (silicate).

The blade edge had been damaged, as evidenced by chips in the blade area, and the gemstone piece was then reworked for different ceremonial purposes. Such rework consisted of first abrading off the blade edge. A deep groove, extending from the middle of each side of the blade and over the poll, was carved and abraded. Further carving and abrasion resulted in two grooves extending from the center of the blade, and following the blade edge on both sides to the original (hafting) groove. Two round eyes protrude from where material was removed, giving the piece the appearance of a head. The animal (fish?) is not identifiable. The piece measures 3⅜ inches (8.6 cm) long by 2-7/16 inches (6.2 cm) wide, and weighs 0.59 lb.

The heart-shaped gray sandstone piece (D) (slightly damaged) was recovered from a ruin south of Holbrook, Arizona. The piece is ⅜ inch (0.95 cm) thick by 1-15/16 inch (2.38 cm) at the widest part. The face of the piece was painted brown-red (probably hematite). Both the obverse and reverse sides and the edge were abraded smooth.

Charm: Charms (sometimes called "amulets") while carried or worn by many individuals, were more often made by or for a medicine man. They were used in various ceremonials, and carried by him in a medicine pouch or bundle, because in the life of these peoples, the medicine man was the aristocrat. The highly superstitious prehistoric Indians thought that charms transmitted magic powers to them from the "Sky People" (their gods) through the medicine men. They believed furthermore that charms not only provided a protection against evil spirits or injury, but assisted in the success of the hunt, war, and in the growth of crops. (NOTE: The general information concerning attitude and beliefs was handed down to present day Indians by their ancestors. Such information is included here for purposes of association only.)

It is sometimes difficult to determine whether certain pieces are objects of a ceremonial or charm nature. To the superstitious prehistoric Indian, it is doubtful that he made any point of distinction between the two. He obviously was confident that either a "charm" or a "ceremonial" object would, by magical power, aid his cause (by warding off evil) when needed. However, by modern definition, a charm might be considered as something worn as a good luck piece whereas a ceremonial object is more closely related to religious beliefs and rituals (see "Ceremonial Object"). Many charms (ceremonial by custom or ritual?) were actually totemic objects, *i.e.,* revered symbols or emblems of family or clan (fraternity) affiliations.

A point of differentiation is made between a "medicine bundle" and a "medicine pouch." A bundle generally contains all of the paraphernalia a medicine man might use. A pouch, on the other hand, is the container for equipment for a specific ceremony.

Many kinds of charms are detailed under the basic alphabetical nomenclature, regardless of the material from which they were fabricated. The following listing will aid in their identification:

> Concretion
> Decorative Stone, Unworked
> Eagle Talon, Carved
> Fossilized Shell
> Toy(?)

The charms pictured are grouped by material and illustrate the variety of such items used by the prehistoric Indians.

Bone: Charms carved from bone (A) consist of animals, birds, and geometrics, and were either worn as ornaments or used ceremonially as charms. They were carved from any kind of bone fragments, which had been cut from large bones, abraded flat, sometimes graved, then usually polished (A,a). Each piece was perforated for wearing.

The mammal metatarsal bone (a part of an animal's hind limb) containing an animal head carved in the joint of one end (A,b), undoubtedly served the multiple purpose of making the piece a charm and a bead. It is impossible to determine the kind of animal represented by the symbolic head. A hole was drilled through the middle of the shaft for stringing.

One of the unique pieces might be said to be the double animal heads which had been carved from a mammal vertebra (a bone from the spinal column) (A,c). The hole, which was used to suspend the piece, is undoubtedly the same hole through which the spinal cord passed. The bone piece was recovered from a ruin to the north of Quemado, New Mexico.

Clay: These charms (sometimes called "**fetishes**") were hand-molded from clay material (B), and generally consist of stylized birds, which are difficult if not impossible to classify. Most were crudely made, though some were well made and even decorated with simple geometrics on a dingy white slip.

Many were perforated for wearing or suspending in appropriate places to induce good fortune to their owners.

The little gray clay jar (B,a), is one of the more original charms recovered. It was well

Charms

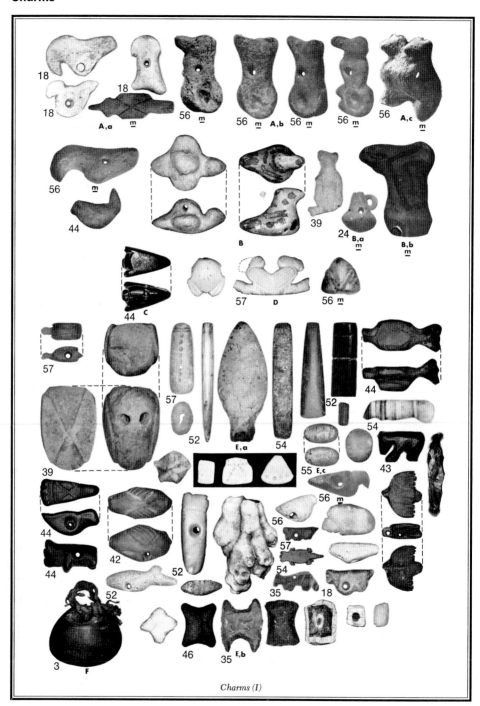

Charms (I)

made, and even has a handle. The piece contains a through hole for stringing in a necklace.

The black-on-gray animal head (B,b) was made from the handle of a Tularosa-ware pitcher. The pitcher had undoubtedly been broken, and the animal-head handle was retained, and abraded smooth in the area where it attached to the pitcher. Thereafter it was undoubtedly carried as a charm.

Jet: Charms made from jet (C), a form of lignite, were highly prized by the prehistoric Indian. The material was easily worked and carved, and could be polished to an attractive lustrous black. Charms made from this material include birds, animals, and geometric shapes. Probably the stylized birds were the more popular, as greater numbers of these have been recovered than any other life form or shape.

Mountain Sheep Horn: This generally conically-shaped charm (F) was made from a section of mountain sheep horn. It is 13/16 inch (2.0 cm) high by 1⅝ to 1-23/32 inches (4.1 to 4.3 cm) diameter at the base. The piece contains a vertical hole 7/16 inch (1.1 cm) diameter at the top, which tapers to 5/32 inch (0.35 cm) at the base. A length of Z-twist

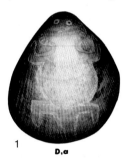

1

D,a

Charms (II)

cord passes through the hole, which provided a means of suspension. There is an overhand knot above the top hole, and another below the hole in the base which prevented the piece from slipping either up or down. From the wear on the cord, it is thought that the piece was suspended for some reason or other (Lindsay, 1968.61-63).

Shell: Charms were worked from many kinds of shells (D). Probably the most prized are those valves of bivalves which were graved and abraded into birds, frogs, and geometric shapes. There is an almost unlimited array of such items. These were used as charms, not

only by medicine men, but were carried or worn by others as well. Most of these charms were drilled for wearing.

Valves of bivalve shells which were etched on the convex side showing toads, frogs, geometrics, symbols, etc., were also highly prized. The horned toad (D,a) shown on the *Cardium* shell is a fine example of the art of etching by the prehistoric peoples.

Stone: A wide variety of stone was used to make charms (E) into many kinds of animals, birds, and geometric shapes. Such stone as slate, basalt, jadeite, limestone, argillite, turquoise, shale, and other local scenic stone was worked into various life forms. Many of these forms were perforated for wearing, to bring good fortune to the wearer. Most pieces were beautifully carved and abraded, and even polished.

The tan jasper arrowpoint (E,a) is undoubtedly a charm worn or carried during the hunt. The piece, though having been chipped to shape, is quite smooth, even including the edges. This condition is undoubtedly as much from handling as from possible abrasion.

The three "pillow-shaped" charms (E,b) have caused much conjecture as to their use or purpose. A possibility is that these pieces symbolize the four directions — north, south, east, and west. Another credible purpose which has been suggested is that such pieces were held under the tongue by a distance runner to induce the flow of saliva. These three were made from basalt.

The small ellipsoidal piece (E,c, obverse and reverse sides shown) was etched or graved in a waterworn pebble. The carved image seems to be that of a water beetle or other small bug. Images similar to this were held sacred by the ancient Egyptians, and were carried or worn as a charm. The piece shown was recovered from the vicinity of Wickenburg, Arizona.

Cheek Plug, see Lip Plug

Chime: Chimes (undrilled but similar shaped pieces are also called "**bell stone,**" and "**kiva ringing stone**") were made from many different kinds of tabular stone, but usually slate, shale, etc. They range from crudely-made pieces to those well shaped and abraded.

The chime (A) measures 13¼ inches (33.6 cm) long, and was drilled at one end for suspen-

35

56

A

B

Chimes

Chip : Chopper

sion. It was recovered north of Quemado, New Mexico.

Chime (B), made from a piece of dark gray slate, measures 10½ inches (26.67 cm) long. While the piece was undrilled, note the transverse worn marking two inches (5.08 cm) from the upper end. This abrasion was undoubtedly from a yucca cord or thong which secured the suspended chime. The piece is very smooth and contains rounded ends. The obverse side was marked (probably with a sharp graving point) with a series of thin diagonal criss-cross lines which extend the full length of the piece. This chime was recovered from a Hohokam ruin south of Phoenix, Arizona.

These instruments were undoubtedly used on ceremonial occasions, and tapped with a similar stone to produce a light musical sound.

Chips

Chips: Chips, while not actually artifacts, were the residual stone material removed from larger pieces during the making of a chipped lithic tool, weapon, implement, or other similar item.

Such colorful chips as agate, turquoise, jasper, chert, basalt, obsidian, petrified wood, or other stone are found in areas where the prehistoric Indian worked and made any sort of chipped items. Chips were sometimes used unmodified as knives, gravers, scrapers, etc.

Chipped and Notched Tool: These tools were characterized by being chipped to the shape of modern single- or double-bitted axes. Most have edge grooves, which were located either near one end or near the middle of the piece. The grooves were for hafting. The blades and blade edges of some contain evidence of surface abrasion, which leaves the depressions of the deeper or larger chips quite obvious. The blade edges of many seem to be sharpened by edge pressure retouch flaking.

39

Chipped and Notched Tools

The polls (if any) were usually rough-chipped, and beyond coarse shaping, were not worked.

39

These implements were a sort of general purpose chopping piece, and were made from stone ranging from shale to any tough stone (agate, chert, etc.). It is highly probable that in addition to the tool being a chopper of some sort, it was also used as a weapon. They generally weigh from 0.5 to 1.75 lbs, and measure from 4-1/16 to 6-15/16 inches (10.2 to 17.5 cm) long.

Chipped and Notched Tool

Chisel: While these implements are termed chisels, it is doubtful if they would be very efficient in the actual use of a chisel, as we know the tool today. They were probably used to split or shape pieces of wood in the forming of various wood artifacts, and for separating laminated or layered stone into thin sheets. Most chisels were from 2 to 6 inches (5.08 to 15.24 cm) long.

Implements of this kind were generally made from bone, long slender stones, or from sheets of laminated stone. Such slivers were abraded quite smooth, with one or both ends tapered and sharpened to a chisel-like edge, nearly the width of the piece.

Chisels

Bone: The bone chisel pictured (A) was made from a sliver of a humerus bone (forelimb) of a large mammal. All projections have been smoothed away during the shaping process, and so true identification of the basic bone is not possible. The tool contains a chisel-pointed working edge at one end, and the opposite end was perforated for wearing and ready use. The piece was polished on both sides.

Stone: The small stone chisel pictured (B), (showing both a side and edge view) was made from slate. It was smoothly abraded, and has a rather narrow chisel edge. The upper end was squared off.

Chopper: A chopper (sometimes called a "pounder") was made from any hard stone available, and was somewhat similar in appearance to a hammerstone. However, it may be differentiated from a hammerstone and identified by a rough-chipped, usually blunt, chisel-like edge on one side, which was used as a

42

chopper. Actually a chopper could be classified as a "dual-purpose" implement — a hammerstone or pounder, and a chopper.

A quartz crystal chopper was recovered (A). It is doubtful that this was a satisfactory pounding or chopping implement. The softness of material is indicated by the several large chips which have been

Choppers

broken off by percussion. The piece weighs 0.42 lbs, and, in spite of the evidence of misuse (large chips), the chopper does show pounded areas, indicating at least limited percussion usage.

Cigarette, see Smoking Tube

Cist Cover: A cist cover (sometimes called a "jar cover") was used to cover storage pits or jars which had been let into floors.

These covers are shaped generally round by chipping and made from thin sandstone slabs, or other thin tabular stone. They are usually from ¼ to ½ inch (0.6 to 1.2 cm) thick. The diameter required depended upon the orifice of the particular jar or cist to be covered. Some were abraded around the edge, as well as on the flat surfaces.

12"=1'-0"=30.5 CM.

Cist Cover

Cloud Blower, see Pipe

Coal Carrier, see Fire Carrier

Comale, see Cooking Slab

Comb, Hair: This three-pronged comb was made from twigs which were bound together with twisted cords of yucca fiber. The ends of the prongs were rounded, either prior to use or from use. The twigs have been abraded semismooth, probably to remove any bark or other rough areas. The piece was recovered from a cave in the area of Phoenix, Arizona.

Hair Comb

Comb, Weaving: Combs of this kind

(sometimes called a **"weaving fork"**) were made from bone or wood and primarily used to beat down the weft during weaving operations on a vertical loom. They were also used to comb out yucca fibers used in the weaving of baskets, matting, rope, etc.

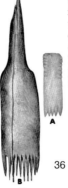

Weaving Comb

Bone: The one pictured (A) measures 3-5/16 inches (8.3 cm) long by one inch (2.5 cm) wide. The five teeth at the one end were formed by a thin bladed abrader, as were the decorative notches on both sides and at the far end. This comb was recovered by excavation from a small Pueblo IV ruin near the Rio Puerco west of Albuquerque, New Mexico.

Wood: This large weaving comb, made from wood and abraded quite smooth, was used in the same manner as the small bone comb above. The "teeth" were undoubtedly cut into the end with a large stone saw (see Saw [C]). The wood comb measures 10 inches (25.4 cm) long. The piece was recovered from a cave in northeastern Arizona.

Concretions

Concretion: These unique charms are natural geological objects, formed by the deposit of any of several minerals within rocks of differing composition, usually sandstone, limestone, or clay. They are very hard and of complex shapes, often having a fancied resemblance to an animal, a part of the human body, or animal or human excrement, etc. They are supposed to have been carried by medicine men in their bundles or pouches.

Items of this sort have been recovered from floors of rooms and from burials of the prehistoric Indians throughout the Southwest.

Container, see Paint Cup; Paint Dish; Dish, Shell; Dish, Stone; Dish, Vesicular Basalt; and Vessel, Miniature

Container, Jar Finger-Hold: These little oval-shaped containers were made from the fingerholds of large Tularosa, Kowina, or Reserve jars.

Cooking Slab : Cord

Jar Finger-Hold Containers

Use of Cooking Slab

Two depressions or "holds" were fabricated and located near the base of a jar, one on each side. They were used by placing the fingers in the holes as an aid in lifting a filled jar.

The ingenious prehistoric Indians retained the "holds" when a jar was broken, and by abrading around the edge and sometimes a flat area on the base, produced a small container. These were possibly used to contain discoidal beads, small seeds, or other small items of this sort, or as a paint cup, paint dish, or miniature vessel. The oval openings (holds) measure ¾ to 1⅛ inches wide by 1¼ to 1-9/16 inches long by ⅝ to 1 inch deep (1.9-3.0 by 3.3-4.1 by 1.5-2.5 cm).

While containers of this kind are undoubtedly found elsewhere, those pictured were recovered from ruins located north of Quemado, New Mexico.

Cooking Slab: Cooking slabs (sometimes called "cooking stones," "griddles," "comales," or "toomas") were made from large slabs of tabular sandstone. They were shaped rectangular by chipping, and abraded on the cooking side to an exceptionally flat smooth surface. Those pictured measure from 8½ to 12½ inches wide by 13 to 19⅞ inches long by 1 to 1¼ inches thick (21.5 to 31.2 by 33.0 to 35.5 by 2.5 to 3.1 cm).

12"=1'-0"=30.5 CM.

Cooking Slabs

When the slab was used, a special fireplace was constructed. Two slab liners (the longitudinal length of the cooking slab) were set edgeways into the floor and extending 6 to 10 inches (15.2 to 25.35 cm) above the floor level. The liners were spaced the width of the slab apart.

The cooking slab was placed upon the slab liners so that both longitudinal edges of the slab set on the top edges of the two liners. The edges where the slab and liners meet were sealed with clay. A fire was built in the housed area, and the open-end construction permitted the tending of the fire at one end and a vent or escape for the smoke at the other.

Piki, a paper-thin ceremonial "bread;" pikami, a fried mush; and other foods were cooked upon the apparatus.

Cooking Stone: These small smoothly-worked stones, though sometimes merely unworked, rounded, water-worn pebbles (sometimes called **"boiling stones"**), were used for the fast boiling of foods which were cooked in water.

Small stones of almost any kind were pecked to a generally round or oval shape. Several of these stones were heated in a fire, then placed in a pot which contained the water and the food to be cooked.

Cooking Stones

Another method of boiling food was to dig a hole in the floor of the room, near a firepit or fireplace. The hole was then lined with an animal skin. The food to be cooked and the water were put into the lined hole. A quantity of cooking stones, which had been heated in an adjacent fire, were then transferred to the lined hole, and the food was quickly cooked.

Cord: Cord, as identified with the prehistoric Indian, consists of thick string or thin rope. Materials such as shredded yucca, agave, bast fibers, human hair, cotton, and narrow strips of fur and skin from small mammals were twisted into cordage. Specimens of cordage have been recovered from many dry caves throughout Arizona. The various cordage twists are quite numerous, and an excellent detailed coverage is referenced to *Sand Dune Cave Report* (Lindsay, NA7523, 1968.80-102).

The cords pictured were recovered from a cave near Navajo Mountain, in Southern Utah.

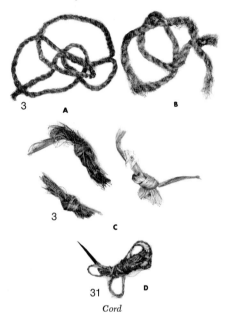

Cord

chips were probably removed by preheat and percussion. Chips were used for making scrapers, arrowpoints, knives, scribers, gravers, and other tools of this kind.

Cornucopia, see Miniature Clay Basket, Imitation

Counter, see Gaming Piece

Cover, see Cist Cover, or Jar Cover

Cradle Board Toy: This name was given to these tubular bone pieces when they were recovered from a child's burial. They were found in a radiating position from the skull. They measure from 2⅞ to 3½ inches (7.30 to

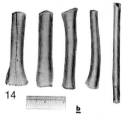

Cradle Board Toys

8.89 cm) long by ½ to ¾ inch (1.27 to 1.90 cm) in diameter. A ⅛ inch (0.32 cm) diameter hole was drilled through each piece ¼ inch (0.63 cm) from one end. The pieces are thought to have been suspended from the hood of the child's cradle board (Lambert, 1954.146 and Pl. XXXV-B). (Also see "Toy[?]".)

Crayon Tube, see Pigment Tube Container

Crusher: These crushers (pounders), each with a large off-center hole, do not occur in abundance in the Southwest. They

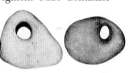

Crushers

are more apt to be found in Southern, Central, and West-Central Arizona. They perform much the same function as a pounder in that they were undoubtedly used to pulverize stone pigment or seeds on nearly flat surfaces.

They were made from hard waterworn stones which were unworked except for the hole. The hole in the light colored piece was drilled and/or reamed straight through, while the hole in the dark piece was drilled from both sides (biconically). They weigh 1.5 and 1.6 lbs. respectively. The light colored piece shows evidence of having been partially pecked to shape, and both pieces show some evidence on the lower edge of use as crushers or pounders.

Picture (A) shows a 2-yarn, Z-twist; and (B) shows a 3-yarn, S-twist. The yucca square knots (C) seem to have been a method of keeping fibers intact and together until they were required for use.

The coiled cord (D) was made from stripped or shredded yucca fibers, which are still attached to a length of the pointed end of the leaf, which served as a needle. The cord pictured in (D) shows a full double twist cord. The piece was recovered from a cave in the Verde Valley area of Arizona.

Core: These pieces are in the same category as "chips," in that they are not, technically speaking, artifacts. These are the residual chunks of petrified wood, agate, chert, obsidian, jasper, or other hard stone from which chips or flakes of various sizes have been removed. The

Cores

Crystal: These are pieces of transparent, or nearly transparent quartz, most of which form

45

regular hexagons, though some are irregular. Such hexagonal crystal pieces are found in rooms and burial places of most of the cultures. Crystals range in width (across flats) from 3/32 to 2¾ inches (0.3 to 6.98 cm), and vary in length. Some small clusters of crystals containing inclusions have been found. The largest pictured is (A).

Some crystal pieces were worked by abrasion and graving, and on some, drilling or reaming had been attempted. However, few have been

Basalt Cylinder

Cylinder, Basalt: This is a well-made cylinder of basalt. The piece measures 1½ inches (3.76 cm) in diameter by 2⅝ inches (6.67 cm) long, and weighs 0.99 lb. The cylinder was pecked to shape, then abraded smooth to form the cylinder with squared ends. The ends show some evidence of the piece having been used as a pounder (hammer) on hard sharp stone.

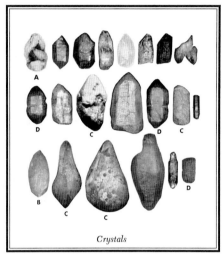

Crystals

Small Vesicular Basalt Cylinders

recovered containing a through hole. Abrasion generally consists of pointing the ends by abrading from the flat of the hexagon (B). Other abrasion involves the rounding or beveling of the longitudinal angles which form the hexagon (C). Some crystal pieces contain a thin encircling groove, either at one end or around the middle (D). These were undoubtedly worn in a necklace, as well as carried.

Crystals are thought to have been carried by medicine men in their pouches or bundles as charms of good fortune, and were employed in their practices, or other sacred rites. They were supposed to have been symbolic of light, and as a consequence, truth. They were also considered by some to be symbolic of fire.

Cylinder, Vesicular Basalt, Small: Small cylinders of this kind (also called variously "stone cylinders," "pahos," "medicine stones," "medicine cylinders," or "prayer sticks") (see Prayer Stick), were pecked to a cylindrical shape, and have slightly rounded ends. Some have ends that were squared. The pieces range from 2⅛ to 4½ inches (5.35 to 10.7 cm) long by ⅝ to 2⅞ inches (1.53 to 7.25 cm) in diameter.

The Hopi say these cylinders are runner's tokens, held in the hand and transferred during a race, much as a baton is carried in modern relay races.

The shaped and rounded ends suggest that the pieces were small pounders or pestles, used for the pulverizing of herbs, small seeds, or stone paint pigment in small mortars.

The cylinders are also thought to have been used as implements to scrape along a serrated guiro to produce the rattling sound of the instrument.

Dart, see Atlatl Dart

Dart Thrower, see Atlatl

Decorative Stone, Unworked: Stones in this category are those odd or otherwise "scenic" or ornamental stones which were undoubtedly attractive to the prehistoric natives. Such stones are usually differentiated from others by the circumstances of their recovery, such as by excavation. Many recovered, which are not indigenous to a given area,

Unworked Decorative Stones

were undoubtedly acquired in trading with the nomadic Indians traveling through.

Of those pictured, the piece (A) is hornblende in mica-schist (from Yavapai County, Arizona), and piece (B) is dumortierite in silver quartz, also from Arizona. Both were recovered from a ruin east of Prescott, Arizona. Items (C), though technically not "stone" pieces, were recovered by excavation from floors of rooms at Fitzmaurice Pueblo Ruin (Barnett, 1973). They are unworked, and are a dark brown color, with varied shapes. Comparatively, they are quite heavy (when compared to similar sized stone), and so seemed to have been attractive to the prehistoric Indian. At first these pieces were thought to be small pieces of meteorite origin, but after investigation and x-ray, were found to be metallic pieces composed essentially of minerals ilmenite, magnetite, and a zincic spinel.

The "pear-shaped" piece of jadeite (D) is a dark green color, tinged with some blue inclusion. The piece could have been abraded, but is believed to be waterworn. The smoothness could have been the result of having been carried and handled for a long period of time, perhaps by a medicine man. The almost spherical piece (E) is also jadeite, but is a light green color. This piece is also smooth and looks polished, again probably from much handling, much as item (D) above (see Color Plate I, Item 3, p. 10).

Deflector Slab, see Draft (Heat) Deflector

Dice, see Gaming Piece

Digging Implements

Digging Implement: The types and shapes of tools of this sort (also called a **"hoe"**) were as varied from one vicinity to another as can be imagined. In general terms, these were hand-operated tools used by sedentary Indians for the planting and cultivating of gardens. The materials used include tabular slate, sandstone, rhyolite, shale, schist, and other kinds of stone native to a given area.

Many of the tools were pecked to shape, and contain abraded blades. Others, less carefully made, were shaped by chipping, both with and without abraded blades. Those pictured were recovered from different areas of the Southwest.

Digging Stick Weight, see Ring, Circular

Disc: Small discs (sometimes called **"unperforated discs"**) made from potsherds or stone, are found throughout the Southwest. There has been some conjecture as to their purpose, though it is generally believed that they were the step (prior to perforation) in the making of spindle whorls, disc beads, etc.

Discs

Potsherd: Many discs, chipped roughly round from bowl or jar sherds, both decorated and undecorated, have been recovered. They measure, generally, 1-13/16 to 3-1/16 inches (4.6 to 7.7 cm) in diameter. Some have rough-chipped edges, while others were well abraded.

Stone: Discs were made from sandstone, slate, schist, shale, and many kinds of hard stone. Thin discs measure from 1-7/16 to 2⅝ inches (3.7 to 6.7 cm) in diameter by 5/32 inch (0.4 cm) thick. The heavier discs (from hard stone) measure from 1½ to 1⅞ inches (3.8 to 4.7 cm) in diameter by 3/16 to ¼ inch (0.55 to 0.6 cm) thick. Many of the heavier discs were "out of round" (almost elliptical). Both kinds were abraded smooth on both flat surfaces and edges.

Disc, Balance, see Spindle Whorl

Disc, Center Perfo-rated: Discs in this category were usu-ally quite thin and light weight. They contain a small hole in the center which was used for string-ing. They were generally worn in a necklace, inter-spersed with shell, stone, and tubular

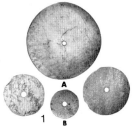

Center Perforated Discs

bone beads. They are smaller than spindle whorls, and are differentiated from them by their size, weight, and small center hole.

Bone: Bone discs (A) were made from thin flat bone, probably a part of a scapula from a mammal. The bone disc pictured is 3 inches (7.62 cm) in diameter, and contains a 5/32 inch (0.39 cm) diameter hole in the center. The edge was abraded quite smooth.

Stone: Thin stone discs (B) were usually made from sheets of slate or schist. They con-tain a single biconically drilled hole near the center. The flat surfaces were well smoothed, but the circularity is quite variable.

Disc, see also Ceremonial Disc, Painted

Disc, Large Granite: Discs of this type were pecked and slightly abraded to an elliptical shape (in section). The one pictured measures 6-1/32 inches (15.24 cm) in diameter by 2⅝ inches (6.67 cm) at the thickest part (center). The piece weighs 5.12 lbs.

The very shape of the piece sug-gests its use in a game. It was possibly thrown, much as a mod-ern discus in a track and field meet. It was obviously not an item of utility.

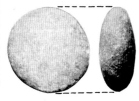

Large Granite Disc

Disc, Multiperfo-rated: These discs with multiple per-forations, made from potsherds or stone, range from the well made to the quite crude. Those made from sherds are the more symmetrical. Those pictured came from widely separated areas.

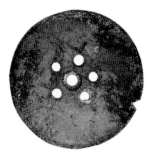

A

It is said that these were cere-monial pieces, and that they were used as noise-makers. A cord was strung through two op-posite holes, the piece wound on the cords, which were held between the extended hands. Then, by alter-nately pulling and releasing the cords, a whir-ring sound was produced by the rapid rotation of the disc.

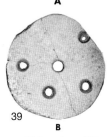

B

Multiperforated Discs

It is also suggested that these discs were used as strainers in the orifice of a jar, to strain out impurities when the contents were poured.

Potsherd: This disc, made from a ¼ inch (0.63 cm) thick sherd from a smudged interior utility vessel (A), measures 2⅜ inches (5.4 cm) in diameter. It contains five 5/32 inch (0.35 cm) diameter holes equi-spaced around a bi-conically drilled hole in the center. There is a 3/32 inch (0.25 cm) deep "V" notch cut into the edge. The edge was abraded smooth and has rounded corners. This disc was recovered from a ruin north of Quemado, New Mexico.

Stone: The stone disc (B), made from a piece of ⅛ inch (0.3 cm) thick sandstone, has a quite variable 1⅝ inches (4.0 cm) circularity. The piece was roughly abraded on both flat surfaces and around the periphery. There are four 3/16 inch (0.5 cm) diameter holes, which have been drilled on one side with a blunt- or bodkin-pointed drill, haphazardly located around a 5/32 inch (0.4 cm) diameter bi-conically drilled hole in the center. This stone piece was recovered from a ruin near the Rio Puerco, west of Albuquerque, New Mexico.

Disc, Thick Vesicular Basalt: These thick discs, which measure from 3 to 4 inches (7.6 to 10.2

cm) in diameter by ⅝ inch (1.65 cm) thick, were made from vesicular basalt. They were abraded circular with rounded edges and flat smooth surfaces on each side.

39

Thick Vesicular Basalt Discs

These were not utility items, but are thought to be pieces used in a game of the nature of "shuffleboard," or even tossed at a peg or into a hole.

Dish, Shell: This valve of a bivalve is one of the comparatively few shells recovered which was probably used both as an ornament and as a utility item. It is a

Shell Dish

small "dish," made by simply abrading a part of the high point of the outer convex surface flat to form a base upon which the shell rests. It was also abraded at the umbo, which produced a hole for stringing in a necklace.

The piece was probably worn, and was also used as a small container for discoidal beads, small seeds, or other items of this sort. It was recovered at Fitzmaurice Pueblo Ruin (Barnett, 1973).

Dish, Stone, Small: These little stone dish-like pieces have often been mistaken for small basin-type mortars. It is believed that the ellipsoidal-shaped dishes were used for mixing small amounts of stone paint pigment, or merely used as small containers.

The dish (A) was pecked and abraded to shape from a chunk of granite. The piece measures 3½ inches (8.9 cm) long through the

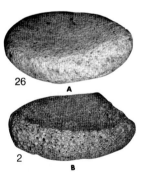

26

A

2

B

Small Stone Dishes

major axis, and is about ⅝ inch (1.54 cm) thick.

Dish (B) was made from vesicular basalt, and is actually a truncated ellipsoidal shape, though approximately the same general size and thick-

ness as (A). Both pieces (A and B) were recovered from the vicinity of Aguila, Arizona.

39

Vesicular Basalt Dish

Dish, Vesicular Basalt: A "dish" of this kind is rather scarce. This item was pecked smooth to an oval shape with an inside opening of 5⅜ by 7 inches (13.6 by 17.8 cm), and 1-3/16 inches (3.0 cm) deep. The base is flat, which permits the piece to sit very nearly straight. It weighs 3.44 lbs.

The dish was undoubtedly made as a container for chunks of paint pigment or other chunk material. The dish was recovered from a ruin in east central Arizona.

Doughnut-shaped Digging Stick Weight, see Circular Ring

12"=1'-0"=30.5 CM.

Draft Deflectors

Draft (Heat) Deflector: Deflectors (also called "deflector slabs") were rough-chipped from slabs of tabular schist, rhyolite, limestone, sandstone, or other kinds of tabular rock. They were generally shaped rectangular, and many of the deflectors have the appearance of a triangle with the top point cut off in a horizontal plane. They generally range in size from 10¼ to 15¼ inches (26.0 to 38.7 cm) wide, by 19 to 26½ inches (48.3 to 67.3 cm) long, by 2 to 2-9/16 inches (5.1 to 6.4 cm) thick.

Slabs were placed edgewise in the floor, and located between a wall opening and a fireplace or firepit, to deflect drafts. They were also used as a shield between fireplace heat and inhabitants.

Drill: Drills (sometimes called "**perforators**") were made from agate, petrified wood, chert,

49

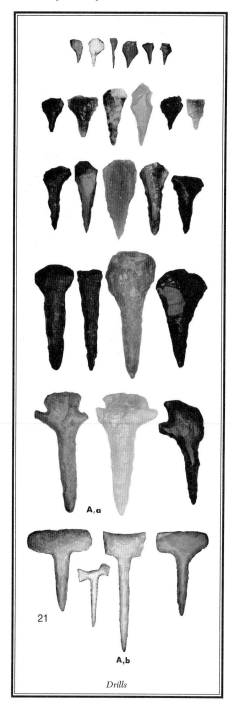

A,a

21

A,b

Drills

flint, basalt, obsidian, jasper, or other hard local stone. Generally, drills, and especially the points, were made for a particular perforating job. They were chipped or control-flaked to the desired point and shaft. Most were hafted at the upper end for attaching to the drill shaft.

Some larger drills were reworked from damaged arrowpoints or spearpoints (A,a). These are identified by the side notches which were usually left in place after rework as hafting for attachment to the drill shaft.

The four delicately worked drills (A,b) were recovered from a Hohokam ruin near Casa Grande, Arizona. Note the fine workmanship when compared to other types of drills.

Drill Cup, see Shaft Holder

Drop, see Eardrop

Eagle Talon, Carved
The three views of the carved eagle's talon show the front, back, and top. The stylized "face" was carved in the back and top. This piece was undoubtedly carried as a charm or worn as an ornament. It was recovered from a ruin north of Albuquerque, New Mexico.

54

Carved Eagle Talon

Eardrop: These are small (except as noted) hanging ornaments (sometimes called "drops" or "small pendants") which were usually worn suspended from the ear. However, they were also worn in necklaces. Such ornaments were usually made from shell and stone.

34
A,a

23

44

56

56

Eardrops

Shell: Most shell drops were made from small valves of bivalves, small shell fragments, etc. Many were carved with serrated or otherwise decorative edges. Drops were round, rectangular, teardrop, square, and variations of such shapes. Some, made from very small valves of bivalves, were unworked except for a hole abraded into the umbo part for stringing.

Ordinarily such large drops as the two abalone shell pieces shown (A,a) would be classified as pendants. However, in this case the circumstances of their recovery indicate otherwise.

They were found one on each side of the skull in a Hohokam burial, indicating that they had been worn as eardrops. They were recovered east of Phoenix, Arizona.

Stone: Small stone eardrops were made from turquoise, argillite, and many kinds of ornamental stone, slate, shale, and other plain stone. Much like shell drops, stone drops were made in every geometric shape imaginable. Many were embellished with simple carved geometric design motifs.

Ear Plug: Ring-type ear plugs are quite scarce in the Southwest, and have been recovered from Hohokam ruins, which are located to the south-southeast of Phoenix, Arizona (Gladwin, 1965.128 and Pl. CVIII). This type of ornament was worn by slitting the lobe of the ear and inserting the grooved portion of the plug. The ornament pictured was made from schist, and contains a series of thin radial grooves in the outer flange as embellishment.

1

Ear Plug

F Fending Stick : Fetish

Fending Stick, see Rabbit Stick

Fertility Figurine, see Figurine, Human

Fetish: Objects of this kind (sometimes called **"animal figurines"**) were held sacred by the early Indian. They were generally used ceremonially as an aid in the hunt or war. They represented an "animal" or "prey" god (animal of prey) which ranged in value from the mountain lion and coyote (numbers one and two) to the wildcat, wolf, bear, and on down through the list of lesser animals (see also "Split-Twig Fetish").

Clay: Crude animals made from various grades of clay were the most common of the hand-molded artifacts. They were also the crudest. While different configurations were obviously intended to symbolize different animals, it is difficult, if not impossible, to identify the particular species of animal which is depicted. Appendages were usually stubby knobs, which do not add anything

to the animal's identification. Some contain traces of a fugitive brown-red (probably hematite). Many contain a 3/32 to ⅛ inch (0.24 cm) or smaller hole extending from the front (chest area) to the rear. This hole was not for stringing, but was included to release air when the items were fired.

Item (A) pictures a fetish damaged to the extent that the head and all appendages are missing. It is thought that missing legs, ears, tails, and sometimes noses and/or heads, were intentionally broken off by the owner, after the piece had served its purpose. This is to deny the use of the fetish to any finder. This piece is pictured to illustrate the damaged condition of most of the fetishes when found.

Note in item (B) that one otherwise crudely-made animal was fabricated so that it would either stand on its four legs, or could be placed in a sitting position.

Item (C) is an odd fetish in that it contains a simulated coat of hair, which was indented with a fingernail. This piece was also dished

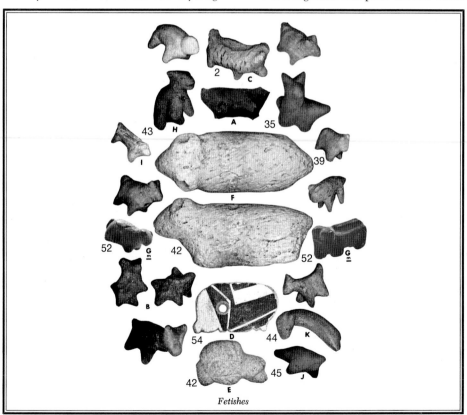

Fetishes

52

out in the back of the "animal," which forms a small container.

Potsherd: Fetishes made from potsherds (D) are, on a comparative basis, quite scarce. As in the case of those made from clay, the animal represented is usually difficult, if not impossible, to identify. The one pictured was made from a sherd of a large bowl.

Stone: Animal fetishes made from stone are not as plentiful as those made from clay. A unique-looking animal symbol is item (E). It is difficult to determine whether the creature depicted is actually an animal or a bird; however, a final decision favors an animal. The piece was carved from a chunk of granite containing inclusions, which form a kind of conglomerate stone.

Item (F, side and top view) is an animal made from tufa, a porous limestone. The piece was abraded quite smooth, and contains a through hole below the right ear. This hole, undoubtedly, was to permit the wearing of the charm. This is the largest of the animal fetishes shown, measuring five inches (12.7 cm) long.

Items (G) were both carved from hard stone. They were quite well made, and were abraded smooth. These were recovered to the north of Quemado, New Mexico.

One of the really different fetishes (K), which resembles an otter, was made from pumice. The piece could only have been used ceremonially.

Some of the fetishes pictured were recovered from Fitzmaurice Pueblo Ruin (Barnett, 1973), and some by excavation from the Quemado, New Mexico, area. The sherd fetish was found in a ruin north of Albuquerque, New Mexico.

Tentative identification of the symbolic animals pictured is offered purely as suggestion, and is in no sense positive or final. Item (H) could be a prairie dog; items (I and J) badgers.

Figurine, Animal: These are simplified zoomorphic carvings of animals, reptiles, birds, and so on, generally made from vesicular basalt (see also "Ceremonial Object, Fetish"). In most cases there are few details of features, which usually makes the piece unidentifiable. However, such is not the case of those pictured, for (A) is obviously a bird, and (B) is a snake upon a rock. The snake effigy is especially well depicted. Even the rattles on the tail identify the reptile as a rattlesnake.

Figurine, Human: These are probably the most interesting of figurine artifacts, some of which were hand-molded from clay material, and

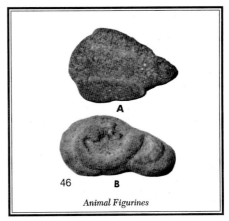

Animal Figurines

others were carved from antler or bone. Sometimes called "fertility" figurines, they were identified with, and represent or symbolize the female, the "giver of life." Again, these are exceptionally crude, though identifiable as the female life form.

Many of the little clay figurines contain a sort of base, though most will not stand upright. This is probably the result of mishandling of the clay prior to firing. A few of the figurines shown contain traces of a rather fugitive brown-red color (probably hematite).

Except for the longest figurine pictured, which measures 4-15/16 inches (12.5 cm) high, the figurines measure from 1¾ to 2-15/16 inches (1.7 to 4.0 cm) high.

The figure on the extreme right in the picture (A) contains a punched neck decoration (simulated beads). This figurine also contains slits for eyes, nostrils in the nose, a tiny mouth, nipples, and is the only clay figurine in the group which contains two legs.

The figure on the extreme left in the picture (B) was carved from antler material. While the

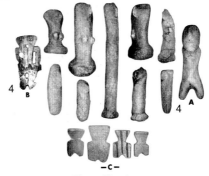

Human Figurines

piece is somewhat crude in workmanship, it was rather cleverly worked even to the inclusion of eyes and toes.

These "figurines," (C) shaped from potsherds, appear to symbolize the human figure. In each case they were well abraded and symmetrically shaped. They range from 11/16 to 1-9/16 inches (1.7 to 4.0 cm) high.

The figurines pictured were recovered from dumps of ruins located south-southeast of Santa Fe, New Mexico (Items [C]).

Figurine Vessel, Animal, see "Paint Dish" and "Mortar, Animal Figurine"

Fire Carrier: As the name implies, this implement (also called a **"coal carrier"**) was used to carry hot coals from one place to another. The piece pictured is a gradually cone-shaped red sandstone piece 6 inches (15.24 cm) long with the cone tapering from 3½ to 2-15/16 inches (8.89 to 5.87 cm) outside diameter. The inside conical hole measures 1½ inches (3.81 cm) at the top to ⅝ inch (0.95 cm) at the bottom. This through hole permitted a draft to keep the coals alive while being transported. The piece was abraded smooth, and contains a vertical handle, which is a part of the piece. The fire carrier pictured was recovered from a campsite west of Wickenburg, Arizona.

20

Fire Carrier

Firedog: Firedogs were usually used in sets of three as stone supports for a cooking vessel over a firepit or fireplace. Many of these pieces are identified by their being smoke-blackened on the approximate upper half of their length, and their crude tapering peg-like shape (see also Pot Support).

39

Firedogs

Firestart: A firestart was made from a large unworked chunk of granite or other hard stone. It has a pitted surface consisting of a series of small holes 1 to 2 inches (2.5 to 5.0 cm) in diameter by 5/32 to ½ inch (0.35 to 1.3 cm) deep. Some pieces have only a few holes, while others

Firestarts

may have as many as 14 to 16.

Small chips of wood or wood dust were placed in a hole. A hardwood stick was inserted, and by rotating the stick rapidly a small smoldering fire was generated. This was transferred to a previously prepared firepit or fireplace.

While these pieces are designated "firestarts," it is also suggested that the series of small holes were made for the purpose of mixing pulverized stone or mineral paint pigment, using each hole for a different color.

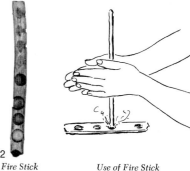

2

Fire Stick   *Use of Fire Stick*

Fire Stick: A fire stick (sometimes called a **"hearth"**) was a twig of hard wood on which another hard wood stick was twirled rapidly to produce smoldering embers. A good fire stick was used repeatedly, and so may contain a series of charred sockets. The small smoldering fire was added to wood dust and fine shavings to build a fire for cooking or heating. The small fire stick pictured was recovered from a site near the Salt River in Arizona.

Fire Tong, see Tong

Fishing Float: Such floats, shaped roughly cylindrical from tufa, a porous limestone formed by deposits in springs and streams, are usually found near good fishing waters where tufa might form.

They measure, generally, from ¾ to 1¼ inches (1.8 to 3.8 cm) in diameter

39

Fishing Floats

by 1½ to 3 inches (3.8 to 7.6 cm) long. They weigh from 1 to 1.75 oz each. Most floats have a thin full groove encircling them near the middle.

These floats were used to support a bait line when fishing, much as a "bobber" would be used today. The floats pictured were recovered north of Jemez Springs, New Mexico.

Fishing Sinker, see Sinker

Flageolet, see Flute

Flake, see Chip

Flaker: One of the few prac-
tical uses of an antler tine was
as a flaker. This was used for
the making of arrowpoints,
drills, gravers, and other projectiles and implements of
that nature. Most tines were
snapped off from the skull,
though many were removed
by transverse sawing. Some
were rounded by abrasion at
the end which was discon-
nected from the skull, but
most were used unworked.

Antler Flakers

The antler point was used
to chip, or control-flake, small fragments of the
piece being worked.

Fleshing Knife, see Flesher

Flesher: This tool (sometimes called a "**fleshing knife,**" "**beaming knife,**" "**rubbing tool,**" or "**beaming tool**") was made from antler points, different kinds of bone, and large chips of tabular stone native to a given area.

A tool of this kind was used to remove fat, sinew, unwanted flesh, and hair from skins of freshly-killed mammals prior to any drying or tanning operation.

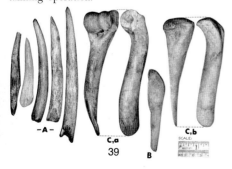

Antler and Bone Fleshers

Fishing Sinker : Floor-Beam Support

Antler: Antler tips which contain a flat bevel (A) might have been used as a fleshing tool or even a rubbing tool.

Deer Ulna: This bone flesher (B) was worked from the ulna (forelimb) of a large deer. The joint had been abraded to the extent that all ridges and other projections of the piece have been smoothed. The distal end contains a beveled edge, worked at an angle to the longitudinal axis of the shaft.

Mammal Bone: The joint of a large tubular mammal (humerus) bone was usually left on one end of the shaft as a hand-hold (C). Most blades contain a short bevel (C,a); however, note that the bevel on one of the tools extends the length of the shaft (C,b). The shaft and joint almost seem to have been polished, but it is believed that such polish was from handling during usage of the tool.

Fleshing tools of this kind, large mammal humeri (forelimbs), have been recovered which are inlaid with small shaped pieces of shell, jet, and turquoise. These form a colorful band of geometric figures which encircle the shaft of the piece.

The larger flesher (C) made from the humerus (forelimb) of a large deer was devel-
oped during the Pueblo III period (A.D. 1050 to 1300). Prior to this the lighter antler and bone (A and B), and even the tabular stone (D) were more in vogue.

Stone Fleshers

Stone: Fleshers of stone (D) (see also Scraper) were made from large chips of shale, schist, slate, rhyolite, and other tabular stone native to a given area. A sharp cutting edge was chipped then abraded along the thin edge of the blade. The thicker part of the chip forms the hand-hold.

Floor-Beam Support: These construction beam support pieces (sometimes called "**beam supports**" or "**notched pieces**") were made from schist, rhyolite, slate, granite, or other hard tab-
ular stone. They were rough-shaped rectangular by chipping, or sometimes rounded at the end opposite to that of the notch. A rather shallow notch was chipped into one end, though on some pieces the notch was located in a linear

Floor Polisher : Fossilized Shell

edge. These supports range in thickness from ¾ to 3⅜ inches (1.9 to 8.5 cm).

Similar pieces have been recovered from many ruins in the Southwest, though more generally to the west central, north and south central parts of Arizona (Spicer, 1936.18; Caywood, 1936.97-101; Smith, 1952.135-136; Barnett, 1969.51-52).

Floor-Beam Supports

Floor Polisher, see Floor Smoother

Floor Smoother: These stone implements (also called **"floor polishers," "wall smoothers," "plastering stones,"** or **"wall polishers"**) range from double-fist size to stones which weigh over eight pounds. The smaller tools (A) were usually dark igneous or metamorphic waterworn

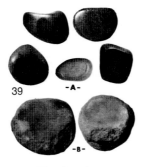

Floor Smoothers

stone, which sometimes shows use (wear-facets) on two sides.

Other smoothers were made from large (six pounds or more) almost spherical unworked chunks of granite (B). These were usually abraded from use on one side only.

Large or heavy implements of this kind were used to smooth floors, and were also used to dress off high spots subsequent to mortar work on masonry walls.

Flower, Wood: One of the oddities fabricated by the prehistoric Indian was flowers made from wood. It is obvious that the only purpose for the fabrication of these delicate pieces must be of a ceremonial nature. They could not have any other value than that of a symbolic decoration.

Large-Petaled Flower: As shown (A) the thin wood petals of these flowers seem to be stacked in series and threaded on a cord through their centers. Note that each individual petal was secured to the next by a small

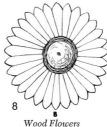

Wood Flowers

thread of gut. These flowers, each containing 10 petals, do not appear to have been painted as the wood grain shows clearly on the petals. The piece was recovered from a dry cave in southern Arizona.

Sunflower: The drawing of the sunflower (B) is a copy of one of a total of 26 recovered made from wood, of which 21 were painted yellow and 5 white. The number of petals on each range from 19 to 36. The petals were set in a groove in a center piece made from a small cottonwood branch, and were secured with a black "pitchy" gum. The flowers measure from 3 to 6-7/16 inches (7.62 to 16.35 cm) in diameter across the petals. These sunflowers were found in a cache in a dry cave in northeastern Arizona (Kidder-Guernsey, 1919.94-147).

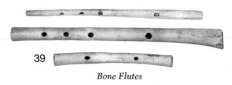

Bone Flutes

Flute: A flute (sometimes called a **"flageolet"**) was made from a section of the shaft of a small tubular bird or rodent bone, generally ranging from 4⅛ to 7 inches (10.4 to 17.7 cm) long.

Most wind instruments of this sort contain a single stop hole near one end, and usually a set of from one to four stop or finger holes. Those pictured were recovered from Tonque Pueblo (Barnett, 1969.104).

If instruments of this kind were played by blowing across the single hole near the end, they are, indeed, flutes. However, if they were played from the end, they would be flageolets.

Fossilized Shell: Fossilized shell charms, made from univalve and bivalve shell, were often graved and reshaped. They were generally carried by a medicine man in his bundle or pouch.

Animal: This animal (A), carved and graved

56

on a fossilized valve of a bivalve, is believed to be a stylized badger, porcupine, or other similar animal. This is based upon the general shape, the sharp nose, the eyes, and the striated markings on the back (probably indicating hair). Many other kinds of animals are found worked in such shell.

Complete Bivalve: This is a complete fossilized bivalve shell (B). It was graved with a single encircling groove. The groove extends from the umbo of both valves, across the convex surfaces and the lips.

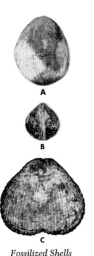

A

B

C

Fossilized Shells

The shell pictured was recovered from the dump of a large ruin north of Albuquerque, New Mexico. There are many rework variations on this kind of shell.

Valve of Bivalve: These fossilized shells (C) are also considered scarce. This shell was recovered during excavation of a room at Fitzmaurice Pueblo Ruin (Barnett, 1973).

Full-Figure Image, see Statue, Effigy

Game Ball, see Ball, Stone

Gaming Bone: Bones of this kind were made from the shinbone of a young deer (see Gaming Stick). Most of the articular ends have been cut off but were not abraded smooth. Eleven transverse lines were incised across the flat side only, *i.e.,* they do not encircle the piece. Only two pieces such as these were recovered, and those from a dump at Hawikuh Ruin in west-central New Mexico (Hodge, 1920.142 and Pl. XLIX).

11

b

Gaming Bones

Gaming Cane, see Gaming Stick

Gaming Piece: Most of the gaming pieces (sometimes called "**counters**") pictured were recovered from ruins along the Rio Puerco and

the Rio Grande in the Upper Rio Grande Valley and in the Galisteo area in New Mexico. They were made from potsherds of both decorated and utility bowl and jar ceramic wares, and from bone and stone. Such pieces have been recovered from ruins and campsites throughout the Southwest, but in larger quantities in the vicinity of the Upper Rio Grande and Galisteo.

There is still some conjecture as to the actual use or purpose of these items. However, a popular belief is that they were used as "counters," much as poker chips are used today.

Bone: The scarcest of the gaming pieces are those made from bone (A,a). These were generally flat and shaped round, rectangular, or various degrees and sizes of ellipsoids. The obverse sides contain deeply fine to coarse graved cross-hatched lines, which were filled with a dark substance which seems to be blackened pitch.

The reverse sides were smoothed, and except for the small round pieces, were unmarked but were polished. A small black dot was located in the center on the reverse side of the round pieces.

Ellipsoidal pieces measure, generally, 1-3/32 to 1¼ inches (2.8 to 3.1 cm) major axis by ½ to ¾ inch (1.2 to 1.8 cm) wide. Circular

57

Gaming Pieces

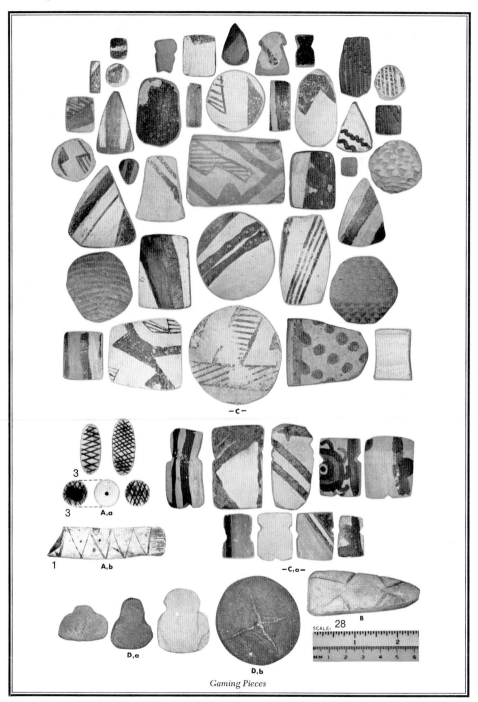

Gaming Pieces

pieces measure 9/16 to ⅝ inch (1.4 to 1.5 cm) in diameter.

The flat bone gaming piece (A,b) was made from a longitudinal segment of a large tubular mammal bone. The graved zig-zag motif extends to both the width and length of the piece, and was worked on the one side only. Gaming pieces of this kind are rather scarce. *Clay:* The gaming piece (B) was hand-molded from clay, then fired. This unique piece was recovered to the east of Phoenix, Arizona. Note the very simple geometric embellishment, which was worked only on the one side.

Potsherd: Gaming pieces made from potsherds have been recovered in innumerable shape and size variations — round, oval, square, rectangular, triangular, tear drop, key hole, and so on (C). Most of the shapes are quite symmetrical, though some are rather crude, with edges only partially abraded.

Gaming pieces made from potsherds of various shapes, though generally rectangular, were sometimes notched in one or two edges, and sometimes even three (C,a). There was no particular pattern to such notched embellishment, which seems to have been included from whim.

Shell: Because of their fragility, gaming pieces, made from shell are comparatively scarce. Such pieces were made in most geometric shapes, generally from large pieces of valves of bivalve shells. They have abraded edges, and most were abraded flat, or nearly so. Many were graved with simple geometric motifs as decoration.

Stone: Gaming pieces made from stone were often shaped into simple geometrics from tabular sandstone (D,a), or other soft stone. The "key hole" shapes of the tan sandstone pieces pictured were found at a Hohokam ruin to the east of Phoenix, Arizona. The round red sandstone piece with the four-pointed crystal inclusion in the middle (D,b) was recovered from a ruin to the north of Albuquerque, New Mexico.

Gaming Stick: Gaming sticks (sometimes called "gaming canes") (see Gaming Piece) were made from sticks of wood, reed, cane, or even worked (abraded) horn material. Some of the pieces were marked presumedly with values, and some with simple encircling geometrics, though most were merely dressed smooth.

It is believed that groups of these sticks were placed in a container, and after wagers were made, a player would carefully shake the container at an angle until one or more sticks were

released and fell out. Wagers were paid based on the marking upon the stick. Such a gambling game might be compared to the ancient Chinese gambling game of "Tin-They-Yuen-Wong." (NOTE: The Chinese gambling game consisted of a "board" containing 80 characters, and a cup-like affair which contained 80 sticks with characters corresponding to those on the board. Bets were made on up to 10 characters on the board. Ten sticks were slowly shaken out of the container, and winners were paid on the characters upon which they wagered.)

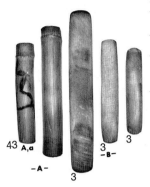

Gaming Sticks

Reed Sticks: These cylindrical sections of either the *P. phragmites* or *Phragmites communis* species of reed (A) (sometimes called a "**gaming tube**") were recovered from a cave near the Verde River in Arizona. These sticks are differentiated from smoking tubes by the septum (joint) not being pierced through, and a total lack of burnt ends. The stick (A,a) contains a meandering encircling line which was burned into the piece.

Horn Sticks: These sticks (B) were oval-shaped (in section) and were abraded smooth (note striations from abrasion on the horn sticks). The ends were rounded quite smoothly. The longest measures 4⅞ inches (12.38 cm) long.

Gaming Tube, see Gaming Stick, Reed

Gorget: Gorgets were small breast-plates which were worn suspended from the neck as an adornment or insignia of rank by a medicine man, a clan leader, or other authority. Gorgets have been recovered which were made from mica and potsherds.

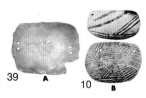

Gorgets

Mica: These gorgets (A) were multiperforated rectangular plates having rounded corners. They were made from layered mica (complex silicates). The perforations not used for stringing the piece for wearing were used to suspend ornaments or charms.

Potsherd: Gorgets made from potsherds (B) were shaped nearly rectangular, but have rounded corners and rounded bases. Those pictured were from decorated ceramic wares — one painted, and the other graved with a hachured zig-zag motif. Each of the sherd gorgets contains two holes, one in each upper corner. These were used for stringing the pieces.

Graver: These little tools were made from obsidian, chert, jasper, agate, or other hard stone. Their general shape may be compared to some

Gravers

scrapers, but they contain, additionally, a very sharp point.

Gravers were pointed tools used to score geometrics or other motifs in bone, shell, or lesser or softer stone than that of the tool. These tools were also used to score small tubular bone in order to break it along the scored mark. This process was used in the making of tubular whistles, beads, flutes, etc.

Griddle, see Cooking Slab

Grinding Stone: A grinding stone (sometimes called a "**rubbing stone**") may be differentiated from a mano by its general compact oval shape and wear patterns.

A

Grinding Stones

Some grinding stones were worked from water-worn stones, while others were preshaped by pecking and abrasion for specific grinding oper-

ations. The stones were made from fine to coarse grade sandstone, granite, vesicular basalt, quartz, basalt, and many other kinds of stone containing the abrasive qualities required for a particular job. All such stones were sized to fit the hand.

Some grinding (rubbing) stones were pecked over part of the surface on both worked sides usually near the middle. This was undoubtedly to roughen up the working surfaces to expedite the grinding operation, or for use as finger grips.

These stones were used for any rotary grinding operation in a mortar or shallow abrading slab, a basin-type metate, and just about any place a grinding operation could be performed, except on a trough-type metate.

With Finger Grips: This grinding stone (A) contains the unique feature of a pair of finger grips, one pecked into the piece on each side.

Groaning Piece, see Bull-Roarer

Grooved Club-Head, see Maul

Grooved Handstone, see Anvil

41

Guiros

Guiro: A guiro was a bone percussion instrument (sometimes called a "**sounding rasp,**" "**rasping stick**", or "**notched resonator**"). It was generally made from a large tubular, rib, or scapula bone of a mammal. A row of close-set notches was cut transversely into the bone. The instrument was played by scraping a stick or a small stone cylinder rapidly back and forth along the serrated surface, thus producing a sharp rattling sound which was probably used to carry a dance or singing rhythm (see "Cylinder, Vesicular Basalt, Small").

Hair Brush, Yucca:
Crude brushes of this
kind were made from a
roughly ¾ inch (1.9 cm)
bunch of yucca fibers.
The fibers of the brush
pictured were gathered
and secured with sev-
eral turns of what
seems to be cotton
cordage. It can be
easily imagined that
brushes of this kind
may have served many
purposes. The brush
pictured measures ap-
proximately 6¾ inches
(17.14 cm) long.

1

Yucca Hair Brush

ornament or charm. Others contain a saw-tooth
end (C) which was probably used as a head
scratcher. These are also said to have been used
as weaving implements.

Another type of hair ornament, which is
totally different from those described above,
was carved from a single piece of bone (D). The
shafts of the pins were abraded quite smooth,
and the joined end contains some simple marks
of line graving. The piece was recovered from
a ruin to the north of Quemado, New Mexico.

One of the more unusual hair ornaments (E)
was carved from a single bone (probably a
large tubular bone from a mammal). The carved
animal at the top is more symbolic, as it is
unidentifiable. Artifacts of this sort are quite
scarce.

−A−

Hammerstones

Hammerstone: Hammerstones (sometimes called
"pounding stones," or just "pounders") are probably the most common and therefore undoubtedly the most widely used implement employed
by the prehistoric Indian. These waterworn
stones or generally unworked fist-size chunks
were of any hard or tough material such as
igneous stone, petrified wood, basalt, agate,
chert, rhyolite, quartz, or other like stone native
to a given area.

These handy implements of the unworked
kind are easily identified by the high spots being worn off by pecking. When high spots or
the whole stone became smooth from use, the
effectiveness was greatly reduced, and the implement was then discarded.

Undoubtedly as the result of either a poor
selection of stone or from rough or excessive
usage, many axe edges became blunted or
chipped and damaged (A), and so ceased to be
useful as chopping tools or weapons. Rather
than being discarded, such axes apparently
were "downgraded" to the category of pound-

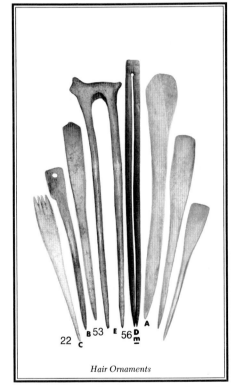

B 53 E 56 D
22 C   A

Hair Ornaments

Hair Ornament: These ornaments with straight,
carved, or curved spatulate ends contain long
tapered shafts. The spatulate end was usually
sharpened to a chisel-like edge, though some
were rounded (A). Some of these ornaments
contain a perforation in the spatulate end (B)
which might have been used to suspend an

61

ers or hammerstones. This is indicated by the exceptional bluntness of blades of many axes (see also Maul).

Hand Drill, see Reamer

Hand Grinding Implement, see Mano

Hand Mill, see Metate

Hatch Cover: These covers were made from ¾ to 1⅛ inches (1.9 to 2.85 cm) thick local tabular stone such as sandstone, limestone, slate, etc. In general, they range in approximate size from 15¾ to 27 inches (40.0 to 68.6 cm) long by 13¼ to 20⅞ inches (33.6 to 53.0 cm) wide. They were edge-chipped to size, and sometimes edge-abraded to fit. As their name implies, they were used as a cover (storm?) for the entrance/exit and smoke hole opening in the roof of a dwelling.

Head Ring, see Jar Rest

Hearth, see Fire Stick

Heat Deflector, see Draft Deflector

Hoe: A hoe (also called a "**digging implement**") was used to loosen soil in a garden, much as a grub hoe is used today. The hoe was a piece of

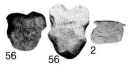

56   56   2

Hoes

layered stone such as sandstone, slate, limestone, etc., which had been shaped by chipping, then abraded to a thin smooth blade (see Digging Implement). Each of the outer edges contains a groove near the top, which was used for hafting. It is thought that the handle was secuured at a right angle to the blade.

Hoop: Small wooden hoops of this kind have been recovered from many areas of the Southwest. It seems that they were used in several games. However, there is some question as to whether

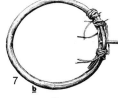

7   b

Hoop

they were used in a secular game, or some ceremonial affair. They could have been used in a game where the ring was thrown at a peg in the ground. Also, the hoop could have been rolled on the ground as players attempted to shoot arrows or throw darts through it.

Human Figurine, see Figurine, Human

Implement, Dual-Purpose: Many of the prehistoric Indians exhibited a high degree of ingenuity by the making of an implement for more than one use. These were generally confined to lithic tools of the workaday variety, and consist of a single piece with which two or more specific operations could be performed.

Generally, a basic implement was originally shaped for a primary purpose, and used. Then, at some later time, a second phase was added to the tool, which permitted a secondary usage. In the following listing of some of the many dual-purpose tools, the primary use of the implement is given first, then the secondary use. Many of these are pictured.

| USES | | MATE- |
Primary	Secondary	RIAL
Abrading Slab	Shaft Polisher	Granite
Abrading Stone	Shaft Polisher	Granite
Chopper	Hammerstone	Crystal
Digging Implement	Paint Palette	Rhyolite
Flesher	Paint Slab	Schist

| USES | | MATE- |
Primary	Secondary	RIAL
Grinding Stone	Paint Slab	Granite
Grinding Stone	Shaft Polisher	Granite
Mano	Shaft Smoother	Granite
Metate (Basin)	Mortar	Granite
Metate	Floor-Beam Support	Granite
Pestle	Abrader	Rhyolite
Pestle	Shaft Polisher	Granite
Pounder	Grinder	Granite
Pounder	Shaft Polisher	Granite
Shaft Abrader	Shaft Smoother	Ves. Basalt
Shaft Smoother	Awl Pointer	Sandstone

Inlay: Inlay work was found on some articles of adornment, usually pendants. They were generally small shaped pieces of turquoise or other decorative stone set into the surface of a contrasting colored stone (see Arm and Leg Ornament and Color Plate I, Item 7, p. 10). The inlaid stones were secured in a partially gouged or reamed hole in the pendant by a cement usually containing a pine-pitch base.

Dual-Purpose Implements

J-K Jar Cover : Knife Handle

Jar Cover: Jar Covers (or "jar lids") were made from potsherds and thin tabular stone. They were made in variable circular diameters, generally to cover the orifice of a particular water or storage vessel. They were considerably smaller than cist covers (see Cist Cover). They were made by most cultures.

Potsherd: Jar lids or covers were made from sherds of both undecorated and decorated jars and bowls (A). They range in size from 2-5/16 to 5¼ inches (5.7 to 13.3 cm) in diameter.

Most of these covers were well rounded with chipped edges abraded smooth, though some were "out-of-round" and have edges which were only rough chipped. Covers were made from sherds from almost any part of a jar or bowl that was nearly flat, or only slightly convex. Many were made from the bottom of a vessel.

39 -A-

39 -B-

12"=1'-0"=30.5 CM.
Jar Covers

Stone: Jar lids or covers were made from thin tabular sandstone, slate, or other stone of a thin tabular nature (B). Stone covers range in size from 2⅛ to 7½–8-5/16 inches (5.2 to 18.8-21.0 cm) in diameter by ⅜ to 15/32 inch (0.9 to 1.2 cm) thick. They were rough-chipped to shape, ranging from out-of-round to subquadrate forms. Some have abraded edges.

Jar Lid, see Jar Cover

6

b

Jar Rests

Jar Rest: These rings (sometimes called "head rings"), made from corn husks, juniper bark, or other plants, were woven or bound together with yucca fibers. Those pictured measure approximately six inches (15.24 cm) in diameter. The rings served two purposes: as supports for rounded base jars and as supports for carrying jars, usually of water, on the head. It is also thought that the rings might have been used in a game of some sort (possibly much like quoits, *i.e.,* throwing the ring at a peg in the ground).

Kiva Ringing Stone, see Chime

Knife: Recovered implements have been made from both bone and stone. Many of the stone knives are difficult to identify strictly as knives because of their shape and dual use as scrapers.

Knives were used to remove tissues or fat from skins, for cutting pottery material before it was shaped for ceramic wares, and for many other cutting and scraping procedures.

Bone: These bone implements (A) were made from sections of large mammal rib bones. The ends were of different shapes, and the edges were beveled. The bone knives pictured were recovered from the dump of a

39

A

Bone Knives

ruin located northwest of Magdalena, New Mexico.

Stone: Stone knives (B) have chipped control-flaked edges, and were made from flint, agate, jasper, petrified wood, and almost any hard stone available.

Many were thin boat-shaped pieces, while others were narrow elongated shapes. Still others were merely chips which were unworked except for a sharpened blade edge. Some knives were pointed at the one end, with the other squared and sometimes notched. These were attached to a wooden handle, much as a modern knife.

Knife Handle: Such handles, used to haft stone knives were usually made from antler, tubular bone, or wood. They were notched at one end to aid in securing the blade in place. Such handles seem to have received rather rough treatment. Most are cracked and chipped and otherwise damaged at one or both ends.

Koshare Symbol: The double protrusions (horns) are the sign of the head or chief of the ancient Koshare fraternity. The piece pictured (A) was worked from a large chunk of vesicular basalt, and was abraded quite smooth. This symbol was undoubtedly used at meetings of the fraternity, and was recovered from a ruin in the Chama Valley, New Mexico. The members of the Koshare appear at all dances and ceremonials as clowns. They wear tufts of corn husks or grass arranged as horns, and paint their bodies with alternate horizontal black and white stripes.

The Koshare pictured (B) was carved by Franklin Quotskuyva, a Hopi, and is pictured to show that there is little change from the prehistoric symbolic clown to the Koshare of today.

Koshare Symbol

Stone Knives

L Labret : Loom Anchor

Labret, see Lip Plug

Lance, see Spear

Lid, Jar, see Jar Cover

Lightning Stone: These matched white quartz stones were rubbed together in the dark, and produce an incandescent glow. They are said to have been used in rain ceremonies by the prehistoric Indians. The glow produced by the action of rubbing the two pieces together was considered simulated lightning, and thus was thought to aid in bringing rain (Stubbs-Stallings, 1958.121-122 and Pl. 27).

Lightning Stones

These matched white quartz stones (A-B) were abraded quite smooth. The upper stone (A) is a cylindrical piece which is tapered at both ends. The lower stone (B) contains a longitudinal trough in which the cylindrical piece fits.

While the quartz stones (C and D) are not a matched pair, they do become luminous when rubbed together. The cylindrical piece (C) was recovered from a site to the west of Phoenix, Arizona, and the troughed piece (D) from a ruin north of Cuba, New Mexico.

Lip Plug: These items of adornment (sometimes called "cheek plugs," or "labrets") were made from argillite or many kinds of ornamental stone. There are many variations, but those shown were, in many ways, similar to those worn by the ancient Aztec and Mayan Indians of Mexico. Plugs like these were worn inserted in a slit in the lower lip, or in the cheek.

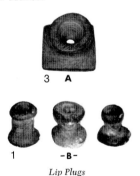

Lip Plugs

The plug containing the large square base and the large conical opening (A) was made from argillite. The striations noted on the flat surface at the large outer opening were made by the use of a coarse abrasive. This plug was drilled or reamed by use of a series of drills or reamers, starting with one of a small diameter, and continuing gradually with larger diameter points, each worked to a lesser depth than the last. Note, also, the drill or ream marks of the different sized points on the inside conical surface. This plug was recovered from a ruin in Northern Arizona.

The three spool-shaped plugs (B), which are considerably smaller than (A), were made from a hard slate-like stone. These plugs were drilled through, each with a straight cylindrical hole. They were recovered from a Hohokam ruin to the south of Phoenix, Arizona.

Lithic Implement Fragment, Use of: The use of lithic implement fragments does not necessarily imply rework such as repointing, resharpening, or reshaping. Such use of fragments involves the conversion of an otherwise useless lithic fragment into a serviceable article for further use. This use of fragments is an example of the conservation of effort, as it avoided the making of a completely new item.

Use of Lithic Fragments

Conversion of fragments includes the making of a small basin-type metate in a partial flange of a metate; an abrader from a mano fragment; a loom anchor (or weight) from a metate flange; a shaft polisher from a mano fragment; a shaft polisher from a metate flange, and many other conversions.

Loom Anchor: Loom anchors (sometimes called "loom weights" or "loom stones") were usually made from any large (10 to 15 lbs) unshaped stone (though some were rough shaped oval). A transverse encircling groove was pecked in the stone near the middle of the longitudinal axis. Note that anchor (A,a) contains the groove set longitudinally in the piece.

Anchors of this kind were buried below the floor level under a vertical loom. A thong or rope guy line was secured around the groove of the anchor, then attached to the lower bar of the loom. The lower bar held the warp strands taut. These were attached to the upper bar and tension bar. Vertical looms of this kind were used for the weaving of blankets or other cloth-like materials (see Vertical Loom Illustration under Weaving Tool).

51 A,a — A — 12"=1'-0"=30.5 CM.

8 B

31 C

Loom Anchors

(guy line) secured around the log to the lower loom bar as an aid in stretching the vertical loom (B) (Kidder and Guernsey, 1919.50-51, 60, 70, 73, Figs. 22, 26, and Pl. 21a).

This large and heavy (61 lbs) oval vesicular basalt loom anchor (C) contains a notch at one end which was probably used to raise or lower the piece with a cord as slack or taut warp strands were required. It was pecked to shape, 22½ inches (57.15 cm) long by 6 to 7¼ inches (15.24 to 18.41 cm) in oval section. The notch is 2⅝ inches wide by ½ inch deep (6.67 by 1.27 cm) across one end (note that it is off-center). The other end was smoothly hemispherically-shaped. A 1¾ inches (4.44 cm) wide by ½ inch (1.27 cm) deep groove encircles the piece 7¾ inches (17.78 cm) from the top, or notched end. One side view of the piece is true vertical, while a view with the piece turned 90 degrees is slightly bowed.

A unique loom anchor recovered was a bundle of corn cobs. These were wrapped with a cord made of yucca fibers, which was secured to the lower loom bar.

Loom Stone, see Loom Anchor

Loom Weight, see Loom Anchor

Sometimes, in lieu of a stone anchor, a wood log was buried beneath the floor, and a loop

---

Mace, see Maul

Mallet, see Maul

Decorated Mammal Scapulae

Mammal Scapula, Decorated: Mammal scapula bones which were decorated (painted) are quite scarce. Those pictured were decorated on both sides with geometrics painted in black matte paint. These items were undoubtedly used ceremonially. They were recovered from Fitzmaurice Pueblo Ruin (Barnett, 1973).

12"=1'-0"=30.5 CM.

Manos

Mano: A mano (referred to as a *"metlapil"* by the Aztecs, or *"mano"* meaning "hand" by the conquering Spanish at the time of Cortez in Mexico) is the companion implement, or active hand grinding tool used with a metate, which is considered a passive, or stationary piece.

Except for those adapted from waterworn stones, manos were shaped to fit the particular companion metate with which they were used. Depending upon the area of their use in the Southwest, manos vary in shape according to the type of metate.

67

Maul

In addition to the types of manos described here, it might be said that manos containing rounded (acute radius) ends were used in areas where troughed metates were more prevalent. Manos containing straight or even down-curved ends and slightly convexed working surfaces were used in areas where metates were flat or straight across transversely though slightly concaved longitudinally. Due to the many types of metates found in most areas of the Southwest, except for the almost flat metates generally used by the Pueblo Indians of the Rio Grande Valley, it would be difficult to classify metates, and so manos, according to areas.

Manos were made from basalt, granite, sandstone, vesicular basalt, or other stone native to the area in which they were used. Apparently most prehistoric Indian households had several manos which were worked in a given metate. Each of these manos contained different grinding qualities – ranging from coarse to fine.

Manos were generally shaped with parallel leading and trailing edges, and many contain finger grips to aid in holding the tool during the grinding operation. Often both sides were pecked to the preliminary shape desired for grinding. The ends were dressed with an up-curved radius to fit the side flanges of a trough-type metate. Others were perfectly flat to work with those metates without side flanges. Thus, it seems that manos are found with about any longitudinal shape or end contour, and made from any stone material available. They have been graded as "one-" and "two-handed" implements, depending upon their length, weight, etc. The general shapes are detailed according to metate types, in the following paragraphs:

Type I: Edges were abraded to produce symmetry. Single grinding surface. Oval to elongated in form. Generally suitable for use with a Type I metate, or smaller versions on the small grinding surface at the near end of some Type III metates.

Type II: The same as Type I, with the exception that these have grinding faces on both flat surfaces of the piece.

Type III: Waterworn stones of convenient size and form, unworked except for use. Single grinding face slightly convex on both axes, suggesting use on a flat metate.

Type IV: Sides straight and parallel with ends rounded. Single grinding surface which is flat along the lateral axis, and slightly convex longitudinally with acute radius at ends, indicating that mano fits snugly in trough of metate. Edges trimmed, and some have finger grooves. Used with all except Type I metate.

Type V: Bifacial grinding surfaces, with one face consistently showing heavier wear. Otherwise the same as Type IV. Some have finger grooves. Used with Types II, III, and IV metates.

Type VI: Straight parallel leading and trailing edges, and each end containing an acute radius. One side contains a single grinding surface. Other side contains two worked surfaces set at an angle, causing the piece to appear as a triangle in section. All surfaces worked flat. These manos were generally worked from indurated sandstone. Used with Types II, IV, and V metates.

While the types of manos described are a generalized coverage of the tool, actually there are unlimited variations of these. There are some manos which were pecked on the working surface to increase the grinding capabilities. Those pictured are typical for the types noted. (Refer to "Metate" for information on compatible types.)

39

Mauls

Maul: The maul (sometimes called a "**mallet**," "**grooved club-head**," or "**mace**"), as the name implies, was a heavy duty mallet-type tool generally used for the rough shaping or reduction, or pulverizing of stone of lesser hardness. Note that the mauls pictured show many shapes, sizes, and kinds. This has led to the varied nomenclature applied to them, which is mostly based upon indicated usage.

The mauls which are suggested as "ceremonial" were made from either very light weight or soft material, which would be impractical for any utility use. These might have been carried as a symbol of authority by clan leaders or other dignitary.

68

Mauls, or grooved club-heads, were generally found in three major conditions: some have heads which were chipped or otherwise damaged, indicating their use as hammers of some sort; while others might have been used as weapons, or as has been indicated above, in a symbolic ceremonial usage. These do not show any signs of wear on the heads (see also Hammerstone).

It is said that smaller mauls were used as maces or clubs, hafted with thongs of tough animal hide, for use as weapons. Such grooved items may also have been tied with thongs and used as a single stone bola.

4

Medicine Tube

the remainder, which was separated by two encircling lines, was decorated with graduated-sized diamonds which form a series of chevrons.

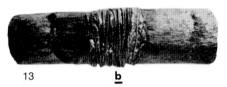

13   **b**

Medicine Box

Medicine Box: This medicine box was made from a 9⅞ inches (25.0 cm) long by 2½ to 2⅞ inches (6.2 to 7.2 cm) diameter mescal stalk (*Agave utahensis*). A 1⅛ by 2-5/32 inch (2.8 by 5.4 cm) opening was cut near the center of the piece. The pithy interior was removed through the opening. When the container was filled, the hole was covered by a piece of rawhide which was secured by a cord of yucca fiber wound around the piece.

The container was found to contain a medicine man's paraphernalia consisting of a smooth black pebble, five paho feathers, and a small cotton cloth bag containing fine seeds (Bartlett, 1934.39-40, 47).

Medicine Bundle, see Charm

Medicine Cylinder, see Cylinder, Vesicular Basalt, Small; or Prayer Stick

Medicine Pouch, see Charm

Medicine Stick, see Prayer Stick

Medicine Stone, see Cylinder, Vesicular Basalt, Small

Medicine Tube: This rather scarce kind of artifact was used by a medicine man in the removal of localized infected areas by the application of suction. The piece pictured was made from a section of tubular bone. It was graved midway with a series of diamond cross-hachures, and

4

Mescal Knife

Mescal Knife: These knives were made from thin sheets of schist, in which small notches (teeth) were cut into the inner edge of the curved blade. A notched mescal knife may be differentiated from a large saw by the spacing of the small notches on the knife, and the heavier weight of the large saw as well as the larger notches (see Saw [C], and Scraper). Also, mescal knives do not have handles, as do the large saws. The mescal knife was used to cut off the button-like tops of the small spineless cactus, which were chewed for their stimulating effect.

Metate: These implements were called "*metates*" by the early Spaniards (a corruption of the Aztec name "*matlatl*"). (They were also called "**milling stones,**" and "**hand mill.**") They came into being for the prehistoric Indians of the Southwest when the principal subsistence, beside hunting, became the gathering of wild plant foods (seeds such as corn, mesquite beans, cactus, herbs, and so on). A metate is the stationary or lower member of the "mill" combination on which a mano is operated.

Generally speaking, there are six major types of metates found. If one considers all of the minor varieties and variations, there are many more. Among other things, many metates contain some degree of rework even after initial use. Many contain evidence of the work surfaces having been pecked with hammerstones, pounders, or choppers. This was to pit and so roughen up the work surface when it

69

Metates

22

19

A

B

TYPE V
(FLAT-THIN, TABULAR)

TYPE I
(BASIN, CHUNK)

TYPE IV
(FLAT, UNWORKED BASE)

TYPE II
(TROUGHED, TABULAR)

TYPE I
(BASIN, TABULAR)

TYPE II
(TROUGHED, SHAPED BASE)

TYPE III
(UTAH, TABULAR)

TYPE VI
(SMALL,
TROUGHED)

39   DOUBLE BASIN-TYPE (TABULAR)

= 12" = 30.5 cm

SCALE (except for double basin and
double troughed types)

30

DOUBLE TROUGHED TYPE (CHUNK)

Metates

70

became worn smooth, to aid in the grinding operation.

Metates were chipped, pecked, and abraded to shape, and made from waterworn boulders or fieldstones. They were made from rough to well shaped vesicular basalt, granite, sandstone, conglomerate, or other stone indigenous to a given area, some of which may be unworked except from use. In some areas, tabular sandstone, slate, schist, or other similar stone was used. Those pictured represent major types, and not variations.

The fine-grained sandstone metate containing the pecked 2¼ by 3¼ by 3/32 inch (5.65 by 8.2 by 0.2 cm) depression (A), is assumed to have been specially worked for some ceremonial usage. This metate was recovered from Tonque Pueblo Ruin (Barnett, 1969.222).

A second metate, also unusual, is the pictured basin-type with the attached "mano" on the lower left edge (B). The combination piece was pecked to shape from a single chunk of granite. The "mano" is assumed to have been a sort of hand rest for the woman using a grinding stone with the right hand. The piece was recovered from the vicinity of Wickenburg, Arizona.

Metates are found in all sizes, and most are portable. This was to permit them to be moved locally. Some were passive, that is, fixed, and were generally communal grinding areas which were worked in outcroppings or other stone masses, or large boulders which were used in place as found. Many of the "communal" grinding areas were located in close proximity to dwellings. However, some were located in the general vicinity of campsites which were used periodically by nomadic peoples. Here, in addition to other foodstuffs, catclaw, dried acacia pods, and mesquite beans were harvested and ground into meal, which was more easily transported than the bulk stuffs.

Reference "Implement, Dual-Purpose," for the multiple use of metates.

Type I, Basin: These metates usually contain a a shallow oval grinding surface, and were made from unshaped fieldstones or tabular stone of about any composition. Grinding was per-

Use of Basin-Type Metates

formed with a spherical, round or oval-shaped grinding stone, using a free semi-rotary motion.

A unique double basin-type metate pictured is the 1¾ inches (4.4 cm) thick gray sandstone piece with edges rough-chipped to shape. It measures 39 inches (99.1 cm) long by 14⅜ inches (36.5 cm) wide, and contains two work areas. One is 7/16 inch (0.95 cm) deep, and the other is ⅝ inch (1.58 cm) deep. The entire surface area was abraded smooth. The piece was recovered from Tonque Pueblo (Barnett, 1969.128).

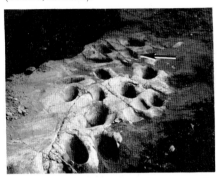

Limestone Basin-Type Metates

The multiple basin-type metates pictured were worked into the floor of a limestone ledge, beneath a huge limestone overhang. In this group there are over 30 metates. They are located east of Camp Verde, Arizona. This is a classic example of a communal work or grinding area. The people who worked here came from a small pueblo located up the hill to the east of the grinding area. The basins measure approximately 18 inches (45.7 cm) long by 9 inches (22.8 cm) wide by 9 inches (22.8 cm) deep. The major axis of all except two of the metates lies in a generally north-south direction. The arrow in the figure points to the only trough-type metate in the group.

Another series of communal multiple basin-type metates which were worked into large outcroppings of malpais is found in an extensive area of malpais (bed of basaltic lava) located west of Congress, Arizona. As there were no permanent, or even temporary, habitations of the prehistoric Indians located in the vicinity, it is concluded that this area was used as a campsite by nomads who harvested mesquite beans and other wild seeds and berries. The metates were undoubtedly used to grind crops which were harvested in the

Malpais Basin-Type Metates

Malpais Basin-Type Metates

Granite Basin-Type Metates

area. A number of large chunks of malpais have from one to four metates. The metates range from 8 to 12 inches (20.3 to 30.5 cm) long by 4½ to 7 inches (11.4 to 17.8 cm) wide by ¼ to 2 inches (0.6 to 5.1 cm) deep. In the midst of the area, the two lizards pictured were pecked into a nearly vertical chunk of malpais. It is believed that these are clan markings. (Note that the legs of the lizard on the left are bent forward, while those of the lizard on the right are bent backward.) (see Petroglyph.)

Twenty-five basin-type metates were worked into granite outcroppings located under a huge boulder northwest of Congress, Arizona, near the base of Congress Hill. These metates vary in size and depth according to usage. A feature is the large granite boulder on which the entire top surface had been pecked with a series of shallow holes (lower picture). The purpose of this is not known. Note the three metates worked into the upper surface. As there are no signs of permanent, or even temporary habitations in this vicinity either, it is concluded that the multiple metates had been used much as those described above.

Type II, Troughed:
The trough-type metates, based upon numbers recovered, were probably one of the more popular kinds. The trough was open at both ends with parallel side flanges, and the grinding surface longitudinally concaved. While many were worked from large boulders, fieldstones, or other chunks of rock, many more were

Use of Troughed-Type Metate

modified on the exterior with round or square bases. Some were worked from comparatively thin tabular stone.

One of the larger passive (fixed position) double metates, which was not part of an outcropping, is pictured. It was worked into a chunk of granite weighing over 600 lbs, and contains two troughed metates worked next to each other on one side. The piece measures 41 by 32-1/16 inches (104.1 by 81.3 cm) on the face. The trough on the left is 13½ inches (34.3 cm) wide by 15 inches (38.1 cm) long by 3-9/16 inches (8.9 cm) deep, and the one on

the right is 16 inches (40.6 cm) wide by 16 inches (40.6 cm) long by 4-1/16 inches (10.2 cm) deep.

Type III, Utah: The Utah-type metate is similar to the troughed-type with the exception that the rather shallow trough is closed by a shelf-like surface at the near end. The shelf, sometimes showing a slight depression from secondary grinding, was usually used as a place on which to store the mano when not in use. These metates were made from thick tabular stone, usually sandstone, or even slate or shale.

Type IV, Flat: These metates were usually made from a chunk of stone, and were even reworked to flat rectangular (and sometimes slightly concaved longitudinally) shaped work surfaces with a rounded and sometimes even unworked base. The piece was shaped by pecking. A lineal stroke was used, with the mano extending the full width of the metate, and sometimes beyond the edges of the grinding surface.

Type V, Flat-Thin: The flat-thin metates (sometimes called **"slab metates"**) were made from tabular sandstone, or even slate, generally from 2 to 3 inches (5.0 to 7.5 cm) thick. Most were flat, though some were slightly concaved longitudinally. They were generally rectangular in shape, though sometimes irregular. As in the case of Type IV, a mano extending the full width of these metates, and sometimes beyond, was used. The metates were light weight, and so were easily transported from place to place.

Type VI, Small to "Mini": The small metates were approximately half as large as their counterparts. Most contain shallow troughs, probably for the grinding of small seeds, dried herbs, and small amounts of stone paint pigment. Again, because of their light weight, these tools were easily transported.

The "mini" metate was usually a miniature Utah-type metate. They were sized to fit the hand, and were undoubtedly used in an operation such as grinding small amounts of stone pigment, or possibly even as a sharpener for narrow-bladed implements.

Milling Stone, see Metate

Miniature Clay Basket, Imitation: These conical-shaped miniatures (sometimes called "cornucopias" or **"nipple-shaped ob-**

Imitation Miniature Clay Baskets

jects") seem to be more in the nature of replicas of Indian burden baskets. They were crudely hand-molded from coarse clay, and were fired. Miniatures of this sort, or fragments of them, have been recovered from ruins throughout the Southwest. While most were undecorated, some have been recovered which were punch-decorated with simple geometrics which encircle the piece.

Mirror-Back, Pyrite: The round mirror-back pictured was made from a piece of ⅜ inch (0.93 cm) thick abraded gray tabular sandstone. The piece is 4⅝ inches (11.74 cm) in diameter, and has an approximately 9/16 inch (1.43 cm) wide bevel around the periphery. The flat

1

Pyrite Mirror-Back

surface within the bevel still retains some flecks of pyrite, with which the artifact was coated.

These mirrors are associated with the Hohokam.

Mortar: Mortars were usually made from chunks or pieces of a hard stone which were shaped by pecking, generally spherical and sometimes ellipsoidal or rectangular. Each contained a cup-like or oval depression of varying diameters and depths, depending upon the kind and amount of use. Mortars range in size from 1-9/16 by 2-1/16 to 7⅛ inches (3.8 by 5.1 to 18.1 cm) and up to 13-13/16 inches (35.0 cm) thick, with holes from 13/16 by 1-1/16 to 8-5/16 inches (2.0 by 2.7 to 21.0 cm) in diameter by ⅜ to 6¼ inches (0.9 to 15.8 cm) in depth. They weigh from 0.09 to as much as 184 lbs. They were made from densely compacted sandstone, granite, vesicular basalt, and other hard stone, and have been recovered from ruins and campsites throughout the Southwest.

Large, though portable, mortars were used as stationary implements in which the pestle or pounder was employed. Small mortars were generally hand-held when used.

Other small mortars were made into rectangular shapes from tabular sandstone. These contain small rather shallow round holes. They were worked by using spherical-shaped sand-

39

39

26

55

Mortars

75

stone, or other stone balls, in a rotary motion by pressing with the flat of the hand. In this way, small amounts of materials were ground to a desired fineness.

Use of Shallow Round Holed Mortar

Many mortars of a "passive" or fixed position variety are found worked into large rock outcroppings or stone floors of creek beds. The round mortar holes pictured were worked into a granite creek bed located at a campsite south

Mortars in Creek Bed

of Aguila, Arizona. In the immediate vicinity there are about 29 mortars which measure from 9½ to 12 inches (24.1 to 30.5 cm) in diameter by 11½ to 14½ inches (29.1 to 36.2 cm)

deep. This site was used by prehistoric nomads and hunters who traversed this area of what is now the Southwest portion of Arizona. There is no evidence of permanent dwellings of the prehistoric Indians near here.

Hard-coated corn or other hard seeds, herbs, and soft stone (paint pigment) were ground in mortars by direct pounding or muddling in a rotary grinding motion with a pestle, pounder, or even a chopper.

Mortar, Animal Figurine: These mortars, made from vesicular basalt, rhyolite, sandstone, etc (sometimes called "animal figurine vessels"), are found throughout the Southwest. Those pictured were made from vesicular basalt. Each contains a small hole, which was undoubtedly used as a mortar (see Pestle, [A,a]), in the middle of a cylindrical piece or the back of a stylized reptile, bird, geometric, or whatever else is used. Many of the figures were carved in bas-relief encircling a cylindrical piece. Some of the mortars are the full conven-

28
46
46
46
38

Animal Figurine Mortars

tionalized figure. The utilization of such figures was also applied to paint dishes (see Paint Dish).

Multiple Scraper, see Scraper

Mural Painting: Mural paintings (sometimes called "painted walls"), while technically not classed as an artifact, *per se*, is a form of art associated with the prehistoric Indian, and his efforts to express himself.

Mural paintings, especially those found on kiva walls, were, for the most part, of a nature sacred to the Indian (Dutton, 1963). Details of such art are far too complex for discussion here. For this reason, the student concerned with such material is referred to suggested works concerning mural painting in kivas and cave walls in the section "Additional Reference Material" found at the end of this Dictionary.

Musical Instrument: The prehistoric Indians undoubtedly combined vocal and instrumental sounds, if only to produce sound and rhythm with ceremonial expression. Based upon the comparatively few kinds of instruments recovered, most wind instruments produced shrill or even raucous sounds or tones, while guiros or drums maintained a rattling or dull booming rhythm.

The following listing is included as an aid to the identity of musical instruments included in this publication:

Bull-Roarer	Flute
Chime	Guiro
Cylinder, Vesicular Basalt, Small	Whistle
Disc, Multiperforated	Whistle, Bitsitsi

Needle: These bone and shell pieces were rather delicate instruments for the prehistoric Indian to make or use, especially those made from bone. They were used in much the same manner as a darning needle is used today.

Bone: Considering the thinness of the bone material used (A), it is quite surprising that such fine artifacts, which were recovered by excavation, have survived after being buried for hundreds of years.

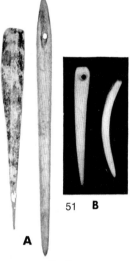

51 **B**

A

Needles

Needles such as these were made from slivers peeled from the shafts of large bones. Such pieces were tapered, pointed, and carefully abraded smooth. While some needles were not perforated, most contain a drilled eye for threading.

Needles, Miscellaneous Materials: Needles under this category were those implements which were made from the points of various varieties of cactus spines, the pointed ends of yucca and agave leaves, or other kinds of

sharp stiff thorns or pointed projections (see Cord [D]).

Shell: Needles made from bivalve shells (B) generally contain a curve. This is because of the convex shape of bivalve shells from which the needles were made. Such needles, while thicker than those made from bone, were well tapered, pointed, and highly polished.

Nipple-Shaped Object, see Miniature Clay Basket, Imitation

Nose Button, see Nose Plug

Nose Plug: These rather curious items of personal adornment (sometimes called "nose buttons") were apparently used by only

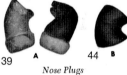

39 **A**   44 **B**

Nose Plugs

a few of the early cultures. While their design may vary from one culture to another, in general, they appear as follows:

A short, round and slightly curved plug made from a clay material (A) was smoothed, then fired. Some plugs were carved from argillite (B). A cabochon made from turquoise, malachite, jadeite, or some other semi-precious or colorful stone was then abraded round and secured to one end of the plug with a sticky cement (probably made from pine pitch or other pitch). A pair of the plugs was worn in the nostrils, probably during a ceremony.

Notched Piece, see Floor-Beam Support

Notched Resonator, see Guiro

Ornament: Items of personal adornment were worn by male as well as female prehistoric Indians, as much from vanity as an indication of affluence. For the most part, lacking a knowledge of the use of metals (except for copper bells), and in addition to painting their bodies with various kinds and colors of paint, the early inhabitants of the Southwest looked to bone, shell, clay, and stone for materials with which to embellish their persons.

Many items of adornment are detailed in this Dictionary under the basic alphabetical nomenclature for the particular item. The following listing will aid in their identification:

Arm and Leg	Inlay
Ornament	Lip Plug
Bead	Nose Plug
Bracelet	Overlay
Button	Paint Pigment, Stone
Disc, Center	& Mineral
Perforated	Pendant
Eardrop	Ring
Ear Plug	Set
Gorget	
Hair Ornament	

It is not only difficult to classify ceremonial and charm artifacts but it is equally difficult to classify certain ornaments which may well fall into several of the above categories. Such is true of stylized animals, birds, frogs, geometrics, *et al.* One difference might be the fact that such specific items which are of a purely charm nature are *not* perforated for wearing or other suspension, while those of an additional ornamental nature *are* perforated in at least one, and sometimes two places. The materials of bone, clay, jet, shell, and stone are the same for ornaments as for charms (refer to "Charm" for breakdown by material). It is noted that items contained on modern "fetish" necklaces or bracelets fall into the same category of "good luck" pieces as those of a prehistoric charm or ornamental character, and are probably worn for much the same reason.

Some of the more fragile ornaments were carved from shell and bone. Probably finer examples of such delicate craftsmanship are the openwork (cutwork) pieces of shell and bone pictured in (A and C). Note the turquoise eyes in the two circular shell and bone pieces. Many pieces of this type could have been worn either as eardrops or in a necklace.

Pictured are a series of representative groupings of ornaments, which are segregated by materials, *i.e.,* bone (A); stone (B); and shell (C).

Ornament, Staff: This staff ornament is made up of 16 interlocked valves of bivalve shells which form a rosette. A peculiarity of the assembly is that pressure (expansion) from the inside of the circular area will secure the locking feature of

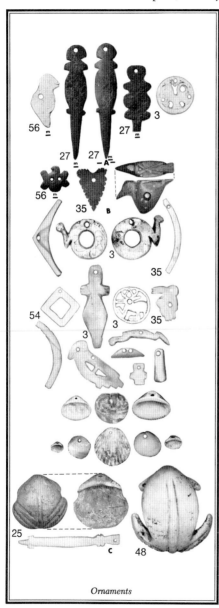

Ornaments

33

Staff Ornament

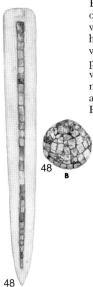

48

B

48

A

Overlays

bi-valve shell, stone (see Pendant Blank, and Color Plate I, Item 6, p. 10), or other material, generally with a pine-pitch base adhesive. Such pieces were worn as ornaments. If perforated they were worn in a necklace; and if not, they were often worn as hair ornaments (see Hair Ornaments).

Overlay on Awl: The awl (A) was made from a segment of a large mammal leg bone which had been bleached almost white. The piece measures 8½ inches (21.59 cm) long. It was abraded very smooth on both sides, and polished on the obverse side. The vertical row of sets are made from various grades and colors of turquoise.

Overlay on Shell: The valve of a bi-valve

the piece to a greater degree. The shells are all of a similar or matched size. The piece was undoubtedly secured (wedged) to the handle of a staff or wand. It was recovered from a Hohokam burial.

Overlay: Overlay was a form of utilizing a decorative layer usually of turquoise, or other gem stone. Small thin pieces of such stone were shaped square, rectangular, or round (see Set). These were stuck to shaped pieces of wood,

shell (B) was used as the base for the full overlay of small turquoise squares. Here again, as in the case of the overlay on the awl above, various grades and colors of turquoise were used. A hole had been abraded in the umbo of the shell to permit its being worn, probably in a necklace.

Paddle, Wood:
Paddles made from wood were used in the "paddle and anvil" method of ceramic vessel fabrication (see Anvil, and Ceramic Vessel Making Tools). During the making of a vessel employing the coil method, an anvil was held against the inside wall surface, while the outside was patted smooth to the desired thickness and contour with a flat paddle. Artifacts such as these paddles are generally recovered from dry caves.

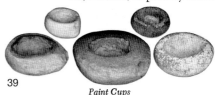

1

Wood Paddle

Paho, see Prayer Stick

Paho, Turkey Feather:
This paho (or **prayer stick**) consists of a group of 14 turkey feathers bound at the butt by a group of seven Z-twist yucca fiber cords. This was then bound with S-twist cordage. The feathers were then doubled back and bound with the remainder of the S-twist cord. The bound ends of the feathers were then bound with a fine bast fiber cord, which completely bound the butt ends of the feathers so that only the cord is visible (Lindsay, *et al*, 1968.78-79).

3

Turkey Feather Paho

While the above paho appears to be of a ceremonial nature, it is suggested that items of this sort might also have been used as ornaments for personal adornment (see Cylinder, Vesicular Basalt, Small, and Prayer Stick).

Paint, see Paint Pigment, Organic, or Paint Pigment, Stone and Mineral

Paint Brush: The paint brush pictured was made up of a bundled cluster of shredded yucca fibers, and was fastened together near each end by yucca fibers wound tightly around the bundle. Note that the brush was so fabricated that it could be used at either end. Brushes of this sort were used to paint any material, much as we use a paint brush today. This brush was recovered from a cave in Southeastern Arizona.

4

Paint Brush

Paint Cup: Paint cups were made from many kinds of stone material, but more frequently from spherical hollow sandstone formations. These were cut in half, and the cut edge then abraded flat, rounded, or partially round-

39

Paint Cups

ed. The bases of some containers have been abraded flat to enable them to stay upright.

Based upon residual traces of paint pigment found on the inner surfaces of the pieces pictured, it is apparent that their use was as paint cups. The inner surfaces show evidence of brown-red and white paint pigment having been mixed in them.

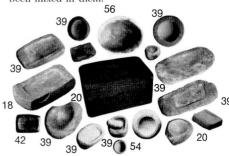

Paint Dishes

Paint Dish: These utensils, made from about any kind of stone, were well shaped round, oval, or rectangular by pecking. While some have simple geometrics, reptiles, (sometimes

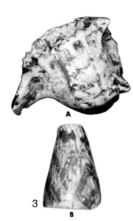

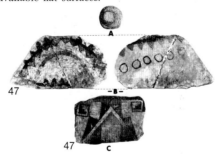

Carved Paint Dishes

called **"animal figurine vessels"**), or other embellishment carved in bas-relief encircling the periphery or incised into the raised rim, others were only worked in the shallow paint mixing bowl or concaved portion.

Large concave potsherds which were utilized for the mixing of paint are classified under the category of "paint dish" (see Color Plate II, p. 83). Such sherds were used for the mixing of paint pigment as were the fabricated kind.

Dishes were used to mix various amounts of previously pulverized pigment with water, which was then used to paint the body, ceremonial objects, or ceramic vessels. Many of the paint dishes pictured contain quantities or traces of red, yellow, black, and brown-red paint in the shallow mixing surface, or dished portion.

Painted Shell: The two univalve sea shells pictured were highly decorated with geometrics painted in red, blue, green, and a pink or buff color. Some of the color has been obliterated from the larger shell (A), but enough remains to partially determine the design motif. The inside

of the shell was painted a brown-red (probably hematite). The second shell (B) is a worked conus shell from which the spire has been removed at the peripheral area (much as a "tinkler"). The shell was decorated with repeated chevrons, diamonds, and a "saw tooth" motif. Such pieces were undoubtedly decorated for ceremonial usage.

Painted Shells

Painted Stone: Various shaped stones which were decorated and show traces of yellow, black, red, green, white, or other colors (see "Paint Pigment, Stone and Mineral"), were, for the most part, retained for use in some ceremonial affair. Many were shaped for a specific purpose, while others are unshaped and only decorated on available flat surfaces.

Painted Stones

The large hemispherical-shaped granite piece (A) was painted with a brown-red color (probably hematite) in a large round center spot, with a concentric band of the same color painted to the outer edge. The piece was recovered from Fitzmaurice Pueblo Ruin (Barnett, 1973).

The two altar slabs of irregular-shaped abraded tabular sandstone, containing the geometric motifs, were recovered by excavation from a ruin in the Middle Verde Valley, west of Camp Verde, Arizona. They were painted with geometric motifs with a fugitive matte paint in black, red, and a dingy white. The series of multicolored geometric motifs on the

81

Painted Wall : Paint Pigment, Stone and Mineral

semi-circular piece (B) are pictured showing the painting on both the obverse and reverse sides. The rectangular piece (C) was only decorated on the obverse side. These slabs were used in ceremonial practices.

Painted sandstone slabs similar to those pictured were recovered from ceremonial deposits uncovered during the excavation of the Pecos Pueblo Ruin (Kidder, 1932.96-98).

Painted Wall, see Mural Painting

Paint Mortar: These small stone mortar-like utensils were used to pulverize and mix various colors of stone pigment. The bowl portions were shaped square, oval, or round. Some were also pecked to various shapes on the outside, while others were worked from irregular chunks of hard stone. Some were found with snakes or simple geometrics encircling the exterior. Many of the mortars contain traces of red, brown-red, black, white, and gray in the bowls (see Paint Dish).

Paint Palette: Generally, these were thin tabular slate sheets on which pulverized stone pigment was mixed (see also Paint Slab).

Those pictured were all made from thin sheets of gray slate, and are from Hohokam ruins located in Southern Arizona. Each is rectangular in shape (though some have concave sides). They contain a raised border which is sometimes plain and sometimes graved with a series of repeated geometric motifs. Some contain a perforation for either wearing of the piece for handy use or for hanging it up when not in use. Some contain carved animals at each end, which were probably used as handles with which to lift the piece when it was moved from place to place. The center mixing surfaces are usually undecorated.

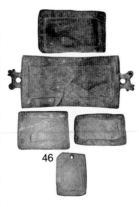

46

Paint Palettes

Paint Pigment, Organic: Organic paint pigment, applied generally to clay ceramic vessels, ceremonial items, the body, and ornaments, was a predominately black color. Colors of brown, red, yellow, green, white, black, etc were generally made from stone or mineral pigment. It is not known just how the prehistoric potters prepared organic paint, but apparently different plants were boiled down to form a thick liquid, from which leaves, stems, or roots were strained away. This method is used by the Pueblo potters of today. Black organic paint (Rocky Mountain Bee plant [*guaco*], and Tansy Mustard) may sometimes be recognized by its penetration into the clay surface of the item to which it was applied. Also, organic black appears as a bluer black than the mineral black.

Paint Pigment, Stone and Mineral: The selection and preparation of stone or mineral pigment required a thorough knowledge of the material and preparation for its use. As a rule, paint pigment was used for painting the body, the decoration of ceremonial objects, and for the decoration of ceramic wares.

Chunks of stone or mineral pigment were generally pulverized with a pestle or pounder in a small metate, mortar, or even on an unworked flat slab.

Paint was mixed with water to form a thick liquid in paint dishes ranging from unworked slabs, to large concave potsherds (see Color Plate II, p. 83). The sherds pictured in Color Plate II each contain pulverized stone or mineral pigment. Note that (A) also contains a schist knife, which seems to have been used as a palette knife for mixing purposes. These sherds and their contents were recovered from Fitzmaurice Pueblo Ruin (Barnett, 1973). Stone dishes containing elaborations of geometrics, snakes, or haphazard criss-cross markings, carved in bas-relief on the periphery, (see Paint Cup, Paint Dish, Paint Mortar, Paint Palette, and Paint Slab) were widely used. .

The Paint material thus produced is known as stone or mineral paint, or pigment, as differentiated from pigment obtained from plants (organic). Some stone or mineral pigments such as hematite, malachite, azurite, etc, because of their intense pigmentary content, were used directly from a small chunk, without benefit of the pulverizing operation (see Color Plate II, Items B, p. 83). The rounded chunk of orange-colored clay pigment (shown to the right in [B] in the Color Plate) was recovered in the "ball" as pictured. The piece had undoubtedly been wetted then compacted for later use.

The various stone and mineral pigments noted here might be considered as those which were more generally available throughout the Southwest (see Color Plate III, p. 84). There were many more colors of stone or mineral pigment materials available to the prehistoric Indian, usually of local procurement and usage. The stone and mineral pigment shown in Color Plate III consists of chunks and pulverized material.

The hardness of each stone or mineral noted is based upon the Mohs Hardness Scale (Schlegel, 1957.219). In this basic hardness scale, the smaller numerals signify a soft material (1.0 for talc). As figures increase, a harder material is indicated (*i.e.,* 10.0 for diamond). Note that various stone and mineral pigments fall into

categories somewhere near the smaller numbers between these two extremes.

Azurite: Azurite is a basic copper carbonate ore, often found mixed with malachite. The color ranges from various shades of blue to Prussian blue. This material was used to paint the body or various ceremonial objects. The material has a hardness of 3.5 to 4.0.

Clay: Clay is a fine-grained earth, primarily containing aluminum silicate. Chunks are quite soft and are found in colors from grayish-white to ochre. In addition to paint

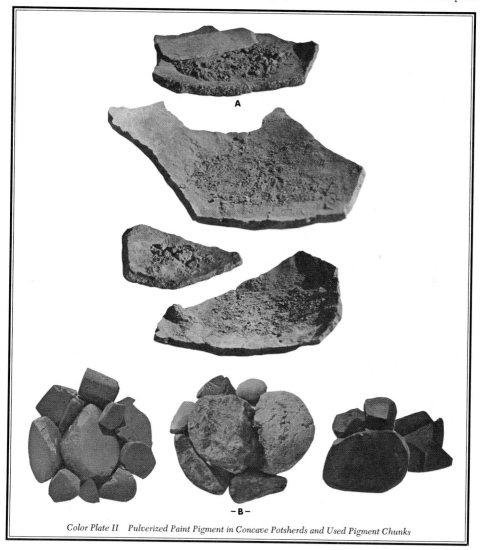

Color Plate II   Pulverized Paint Pigment in Concave Potsherds and Used Pigment Chunks

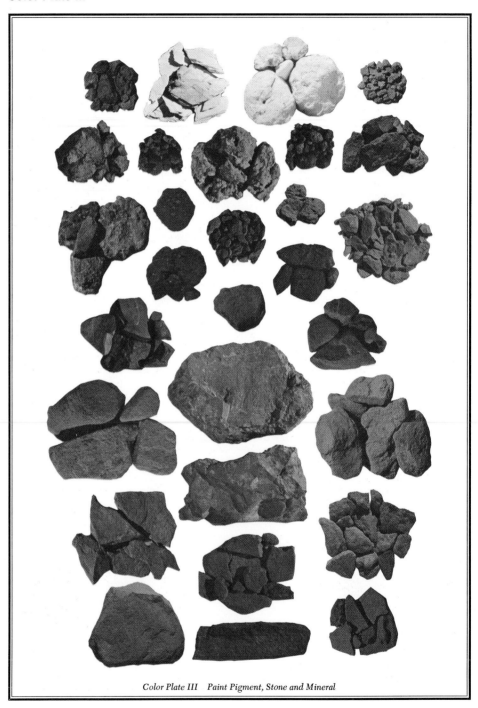

Color Plate III   Paint Pigment, Stone and Mineral

pigment, the material was used as a base for ceramic vessels and other clay items.

Gypsum: Gypsum is a chalky hydrated sulfate of calcium which is quite soft (hardness 1.5 to 2.0). It ranges in color from a dingy off-white (grayish) to a light beige. This material was used as a body paint for ceremonials and for decoration on some ceramic wares.

Hematite: Of all the stone paint pigments, hematite was undoubtedly the most widely used. The material is a brown-red color of nonmetallic anhydrous iron sesquoxide containing exceptionally intense pigment. It is more readily soluble in water than most pigments, and has a hardness of 5.5 to 6.4. It is found throughout most of the Southwest.

Kaolin: Kaolin is a fine white clay — a hydrous aluminum silicate. The material is as soft as gypsum (1.5 to 2.0), and produces a rather dingy white. It was used to paint the body for ceremonials, and for decoration on ceramic wares.

Limonite: Limonite is an iron ore which is a yellowish-brown color (60 per cent iron) found in many rocks and clay. It was used to paint ceremonial objects. Limonite has a hardness of 1.0 to 5.5.

Malachite: Malachite is a basic copper carbonate producing a bluish-green color. It has a hardness of 3.5 to 4.0. It is believed that this material was used exclusively for the decoration of objects for ceremonial usage.

Sandstone: Sandstone is a sedimentary stone found in many colors, such as brown-red, red, orange, yellow, gray, and salmon. It is easy to understand why the material seems to have been a favorite of the prehistoric Indian. Not only the colors, but the availability of the stone added to its attractiveness. Chunks of the colors noted and variations of these, have been recovered by excavation from ruins throughout the Southwest.

Paint Slab: Slabs of this kind were unworked flat slabs. Sometimes chunks of any kind of stone with a flat surface were used as an expedient. Various kinds and colors of stone pigment were

12"=1'-0"=30.5 CM.

Paint Slabs

mixed with water on these surfaces prior to application to the body, ceramic wares, ceremonial objects, and wherever else desired.

Slabs are often identified by splotches of color found on a flat surface. Hematite (brown-

red) is more apt to be seen than most, as the pigment has a very high degree of intensity so that the color remains on whatever stone was used. However, yellow, red, black, and sometimes green matte paint also often remains on stones of a slightly porous nature.

39

Palette Knives

Palette Knife: These tools were made from thin tapering chips of slate, rhyolite, or other similar layered stone. They were usually shaped by chipping, generally similar in form to a modern axe head. The blade part was abraded to a thin semi-sharp edge.

Spatulate bladed palette knives of this sort were used to mix pulverized and wetted stone pigment on a paint palette or slab.

Pendant: These hanging ornaments were usually worn in a necklace. They are differentiated from eardrops by their being considerably larger and consequently heavier (see also Eardrop). They are similar in shape to eardrops, being square, round, oval, rectangular, tear drop, or cylindrical. They were made from potsherds, shell, and an unlimited variety of semiprecious and gem stones, in addition to any and every kind of decorative and scenic stone. All pendants were perforated with one or two holes for suspending.

Bone: Bone pendants (A) are quite scarce. Like discoidal bone beads, pendants were usually made from rather thin sheets of bone sliced from large tubular mammal bone. They were normally made rectangular in shape with rounded corners, and many were carved with simple geometrics. They were perforated at one end and abraded on both sides and the peripheral edge.

Jet: Jet, a kind of lignite, could be polished to a lustrous black. Because of the tendency of some of the material to fracture when dried out over a period of time, jet was not

85

Pendants I

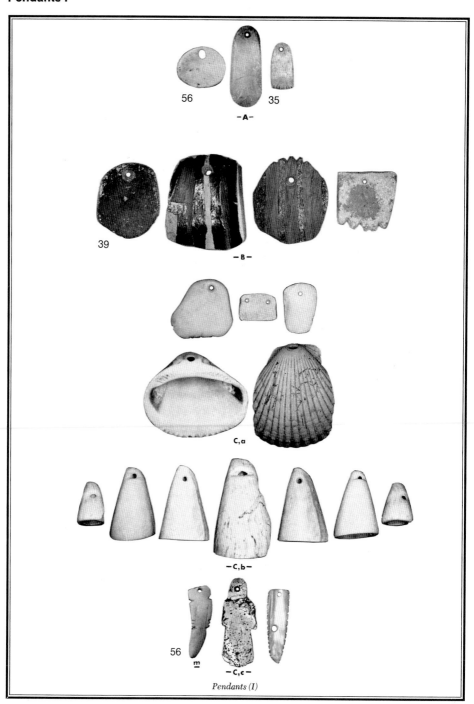

Pendants (I)

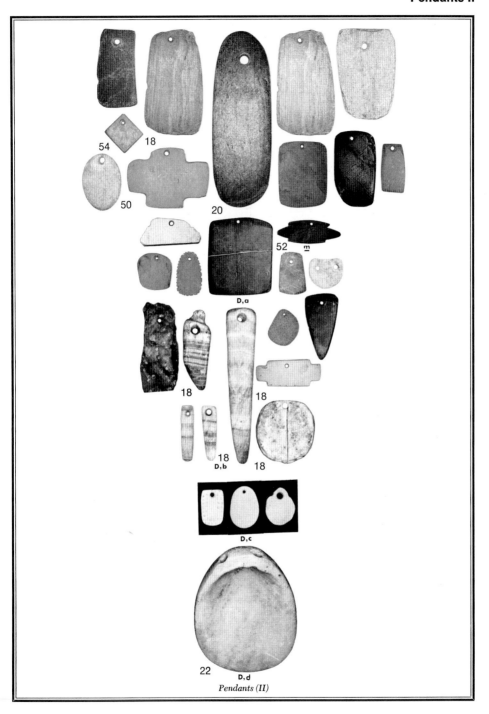

Pendants (II)

used for items of adornment to any great extent.

Jet pendants were abraded smooth and were made in many geometric shapes. They were perforated with a single hole at one end for wearing in a necklace.

Potsherd: Pendants made from potsherds (B) were not prevalent. They were generally made from fragments of decorated ceramic vessels, though some were made from corrugated or other undecorated ceramic ware sherds. Some were worked from edge pieces of vessels. They were shaped according to the sherd used. Most have edges which have been abraded smooth, though some were only rough abraded. A few have been recovered with a series of saw-tooth notches cut into an edge for additional decoration. All were perforated for wearing in a necklace.

Shell: Shell pendants (C,a) were considerably larger than shell drops, though they were similarly shaped — round, square, rectangular, and many exotic shapes. They were usually made from the single valve of bi-valve shells, and were abraded at the umbo part to produce a hole for stringing. Edges were sometimes notched for embellishment.

Many various size conus shells were cut transversely at the periphery, which produced a bell-shaped piece called a "tinkler" (C,b). A cut was made in the side near the end of the canal part to make a hole for stringing. Such shell tinklers were usually worn in clusters on the arms or legs and when rattled together produced a light clinking sound which aided in the cadence of the measured movements of a dance, whether ceremonial or otherwise (see Rattle, Deer Hoof, or Tinkler, Bone).

Many shell pendants were graved and were embellished with irregular-cut geometrics and shapes (C,c).

Stone: Pendants were made from any kind of stone (D), in addition to gem, semiprecious, or scenic, though turquoise and argillite seemed to be the most popular. Pendants are found with graved geometrics, criss-cross patterns, etc, on just about any shape stone (D,a). Also, many contain turquoise inlay (see Color Plate I, Item 6, p. 10). Pendants made from banded calcite, honey onyx, etc, seem to be the only cylindrical-shaped ornaments of that type (D,b). The three white pendants on the black background (D,c) and the large shell-shaped pendant (D,d) are the only pendants in the group which are made from limestone.

While most stone pendants were perforated

with a single hole for wearing in a necklace, some were perforated with two holes.

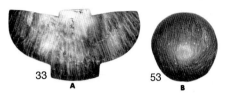

Pendant Blanks

Pendant Blank: These pendant blanks were variously shaped from wood, shell and different kinds of stone. The blanks were used to hold an overlay of small, shaped pieces of semiprecious and other colorful stones (see Set), and were pendants in necklaces.

Shell: The shell overlay blank (A) was shaped like a bird with outspread wings. The ornament piece was carved from a large flattish segment of the valve of a bivalve shell. The piece was recovered from a Hohokam burial located to the east of Casa Grande, Arizona. The square turquoise overlay pieces were recovered with the shell, but had fallen away from the shell blank many centuries ago.

Stone: The stone blank shown (B) was actually hemispherically shaped, with the reverse side hollowed out. The piece was beautifully made from argillite. Note the hole at the top for wearing as a pendant. The striations are from coarse abrasion during the shaping of the blank.

Pendant, Small, see Eardrop

Perforator, see Drill, Awl, or Punch

Pestle: These are tools used to pound or grind seeds, mesquite beans, corn, paint pigment, or other substances in a mortar. They were made from any kind of hard stone, and were shaped

Pestles

generally cylindrical, with ends usually rounded from use as a pounder.

The inverted mushroom-shaped pestle (A,a) was recovered with a vesicular basalt mortar (see Animal Figurine Mortar) south of Phoenix, Arizona. The pestle (A,b), also made from vesicular basalt, is a variation of (A,a).

The two round, vesicular basalt, spool-shaped pestles (B) were both well made, even to the extent of smooth abrasion. The longest of the two measures 4½ inches (11.33 cm). The lack of any wear at the ends of either piece probably indicates they were unused or reworked. They were recovered in the area east of Phoenix, Arizona.

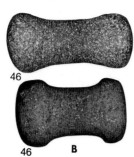

46

46   **B**

Spool-Shaped Pestles

Petroglyph: Petroglyphs (often called "**rock carvings**") are prehistoric carvings or inscriptions "pecked" with hammerstones or choppers, usually into large rocks. Such markings consist of geometrics, reptiles, symbolized animals, etc. Markings of this kind are often found on large outcroppings and fieldstones of basalt, granite, sandstone, or other local exposed stone.

The volute pictured on the small granite stone (A) was found south of Phoenix, Arizona.

The petroglyphs on the granite stone (B) are a series of interlocking meandering sinuous lines which seem to have no beginning or ending. Some of the motifs actually make interlocking scrolls.

The main marking on the granite stone (C) consists of an outlined simple avellan (plain) cross on a rather undulating surface. Other markings appear on the elongated face, but they seem to be rather random markings.

The petroglyphs pictured in (D) are a representative group of those which were found on a hillside at the foot of the Big Horn Mountain range 24 miles (38.64 km) southeast of Aguila, Arizona. The area is covered with an extensive grouping of large, irregular, desert varnish-covered chunks of basalt. Those rocks with the pecked markings seemed to follow an approximately 20-foot (7.0 m) wide space up the hillside. There were no other marked rocks found in the immediate vicinity. The pecked markings consist of inscribed random symbols, male and female line figures, aimlessly mean-

dering sinuous lines, reptiles, volutes, and many more. (Note on the upper left rock picture in series [D] the plain outlined cross. This motif is almost identical to that found on the large granite boulder on item [C]. A cross of this kind is said to indicate a crossing of trails.)

The petroglyphs in (D) were undoubtedly the work of nomadic Indians. There is no existing evidence of dwellings or even a campsite in the vicinity.

Pictographs, often miscalled "petroglyphs," generally consist of prehistoric drawings or paintings on a rock wall (as in a cave). They are usually pictorial representations of objects used to symbolize a story or action.

Pictograph, see Petroglyph

Pigment Stick: This pencil-like pigment stick (A) was used in conjunction with a small concretion-like chunk (B) which has been coated with azurite. The cylindrical

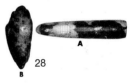

A

28

B

Pigment Stick

stick part of the ensemble seems to be composed of a combination of indurated clay and azurite substance. The stick, when in use, was twisted into a recessed hole in the chunk material with a rapid clockwise-counterclockwise motion. This action ground off small quantities of material from the stick and chunk which produced a bluish-colored powder (see Paint Pigment, Stone and Mineral) which, in turn, was mixed with water and used as needed.

Pigment Tube Container: These containers for pulverized stone and mineral pigment (sometimes called a "**crayon tube**") were 5 to 6 inches (12.70 to 15.24 cm) long, and were made from *Pragmites communis* or sometimes *P. pragmites* species of reed cane. The base of the piece is the septum, or inside wall or partition which is formed by the outside node from which the leaf or leaves once grew. When the container was filled with powdered pigment, a plug or stopper of wood or cotton was employed to block up the open end (see Gaming Stick (A), which is similar to the tube container).

Pin: Pins made from bone (generally about 2½ to 3⅞ inches [6.4 to 9.8 cm] long) are cylindrical or only very slightly tapered in shape, and have either quite blunt or rounded ends. They were abraded smooth and were highly polished. While their actual use is not known, it is sug-

89

Petroglyphs

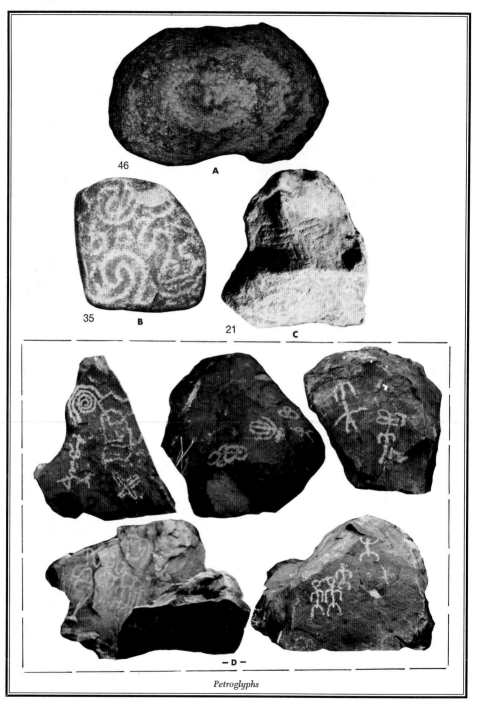

Petroglyphs

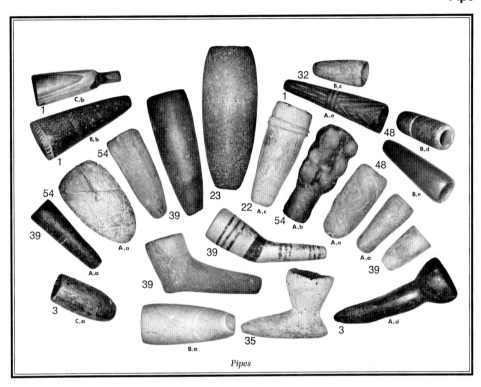

Pipes

gested that they might have been worn in the hair, much as hairpins today. Traces of the original kind of bone are obliterated because of the shaping by abrasion.

Pipe: Pipes (sometimes called "**smoke blowers**" or "**cloud blowers**") were in use by most of the cultures throughout the Southwest by circa A.D. 1300. It is said that pipes were only used ceremonially at that time. The earliest pipes were the "straight" tubular or cylindrical kind, tapering slightly from the bowl end toward the stem, similar to modern day cigar holders. They were smoked in a reclining position, or with a hollow straw or reed inserted into the small end.

At a later date, circa A.D. 1400, pipes with bowls and an approximately 30° bend in the short stem came into being. Many of these were painted with black or brown matte paint decoration, on an off-white slip base. The decorations usually consisted of encircling rings or simple geometrics. The 90° elbow stem with a larger bowl followed. The bent stemmed pipes during

39

Bone Pins

this time were also smoked through a straw (Switzer, 1969).

The largest pipe of those pictured measures 3¾ inches (9.5 cm) long.

Clay Material: These pipes (A) were hand-molded from tan, red, and gray clay material. Most of them measure between 1⅛ and 3 inches (2.8 and 7.5 cm) long. Some pipes have painted, punched, or graved ornamentation, or a combination of these. This usually consists of simple geometric motifs of every description which either encircles or extends the longitudinal length of the pipe (A,a). Additionally, embellishment was formed by finger pressing the clay into a series of protruding halfmoon or other similar motifs (A,b). Some contain simple appliqued ornamentation (A,c). However, many pipes were without any embellishment, and were smooth-shaped round or square.

Of those pictured, note that one contains three simple graved encircling lines. Another contains an encircling graved and punched ornamental motif, while still another contains graved longitudinal sinuous lines which extend in repeated series around the entire

91

periphery. Others contain hand-molded adornment.

The black clay pipe with the slightly curved stem and flared bowl (A,d) is one of the more unusual which was recovered. It measures 3⅛ inches (7.93 cm) long.

The slender painted pipe (A,e) is a black-on-gray of an Anasazi Culture ware. Narrow lines are painted from the mouthpiece to the three lines encircling the middle of the pipe. The design motif from these three lines to the bowl end consists of a series of chevrons with short dashes separating them. All design motifs completely cover the exterior.

Stone: Tubular pipes were also found made from stone, generally scenic (B,a), or other ornamental stone such as epidote (B,b), argillite, limestone (B,c), etc. While most were abraded smooth, some contain simple graved geometric motifs. Though most stone pipes are round, some are found which have been abraded square.

The pipe (B,d) was made from jadeite, and contains a single encircling groove as embellishment. It measures 1-15/16 inches (4.92 cm) long. Pipe (B,e) was made from argillite, and measures 2⅝ inches (6.67 cm) long. It does not contain any decoration, just a very high polish.

Wood: Cylindrical pipes made of wood are considered a rarity. The one pictured (C,a) measures 1⅝ inches (4.12 cm) long by 13/16 inch (2.06 cm) diameter. There is only a slight polish as a finish, no graving or other elaboration on the piece.

The wood pipe (C,b) has a smoothed shaft and bowl end, and contains a small reed mouthpiece which was inserted into the shaft. It was secured in place with a solid black material, which seems to be a clay mixture. Except for the grain of the wood showing clearly, there is no embellishment on the pipe.

Plain Tube, see Bead (Tubular Bone)

Planting Implement: These tools made from various kinds of stone are rather scarce, as most planting tools were made from wood. The planting implement pictured measures 13 inches (32.0 cm) long. It was well shaped from a chunk of slate, has a handle and sharp point, and was abraded quite smooth. This piece was recovered from a campsite west of Wickenburg, Arizona.

20
*Planting
Implement*

When used, the implement was poked into the ground, and the seed dropped into the hole, then covered. A similar method is used today, except that a dibble is employed to prepare the hole.

Planting Stick: These were usually heavy sticks of varying diameters, which range from 30 to 40 inches (76.2 to 101.6 cm) long. They were sharpened at one end with a bodkin-type point. A circular stone ring was wedged near the pointed end of the stick as a "stop" and stick weight, to insure a desired uniform depth of penetration in the ground for the planting of seeds (see Ring, Circular).

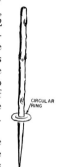

CIRCULAR RING

Plaque: This unfired plaque was made from a fine grade of clay material. The surface is quite smooth, and contains a semi-polish, as though from a considerable amount of hand rubbing, or just handling.

Planting Stick

The piece pictured measures 5-3/16 by 4 by ½ inch (13.0 by 10.2 by 1.3 cm). The two 5/32 inch (0.39 cm) diameter holes were located ½ inch (1.27 cm) from one longitudinal edge and were spaced 2-9/16 inches (6.5 cm) apart.

39
Plaque

While the actual use of the item is not known, it is thought that the configuration suggests a "prayer" plaque or talisman. The piece may have been suspended in a kiva or walkway, or even in a room, and may have had some ceremonial use or significance.

The plaque pictured was recovered from the top of a stone slab which had been placed over an infant's burial, and located under the floor of a room at a site to the northwest of Albuquerque, New Mexico.

Plastering Stone: These were stones, usually thick and rectangular in shape, which contained an extended finger groove on each side, paralleling the longitudinal axis. While most were made from sandstone, some were made from granite, vesicular basalt, or other hard stone. These plastering, or rubbing, stones weigh from 5.56 to 11.12 lbs each. They were used to smooth or dress off masonry or adobe walls and floors. Many of these stones are found with wall or floor clay material still adhering to them (see Floor Smoother).

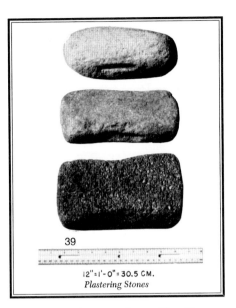

39

12"=1'-0"=30.5 CM.
Plastering Stones

Plug, see Ear Plug, Lip Plug, or Nose Plug

Plume Holder (?): This peculiar-looking piece was made from a chunk of tufa. The handle and bowl suggest a plume (feather) holder or carrier.

The item measures 4⅞ inches (12.38 cm) long.

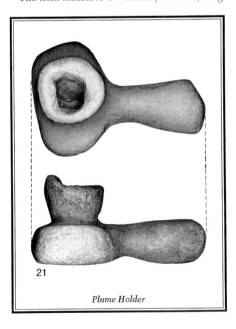

21

Plume Holder

Polishing Stones

The bowl is nearly the depth of the thickness of the piece. The entire surface was abraded quite smooth. There are no holes, either through the handle or through the bottom of the bowl.

Polishing Stone: These little implements (sometimes called "smoothing stones") are unmodified except from use. They were usually a hard waterworn igneous stone, and are identified by one or more worn (almost polished) surfaces, which may be flat, convex, or even concaved.

These implements were used to smooth and polish the wetted surfaces of vessels during the fabrication of ceramic wares and before firing. Many of the Indian potters of today still employ the use of polishing stones to dress off pottery wares, or to give such pieces added polish.

Pot Stopper: These crude pot stoppers (sometimes called "pot seals," "pot lids," or "clay stoppers") were made from a coarse clay. They

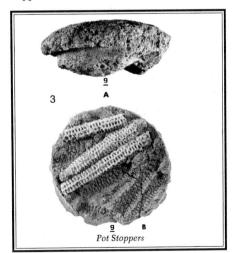

3

9
A

9   B

Pot Stoppers

93

Pot Stopper : Pottery Smoothing Implement

seemed to have been made by the simple expedient of forcing a portion of wet clay into a jar opening, then withdrawing it for drying. In this manner, such covers were made to fit the opening of a specic jar. The cover (A) measures 3-5/16 inches (8.3 cm) in diameter. The cover (B) shows the underside of a second cover which measures 3⅜ inches (8.5 cm) in diameter. It had been pushed into the orifice of a jar which was filled with corn, some of which adhered to the wet clay when the cover was being fitted. The top, or upper side, is smooth and convex (Lindsay, *et al*, 1968.55).

Pot Lid, see Pot Stopper

Pot Seal, see Pot Stopper

Potsherd, see Sherd

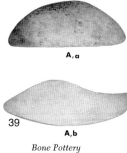

A,a

A,b

39

Bone Pottery Smoothing Implements

Bone: These were made from pieces of flat mammal bone (probably a part of a scapula). They were generally kidney shaped, with the edges abraded smooth. Tools of this kind were quite delicate, and difficult to recover.

In the picture, implement (A,a) was recovered from a ruin north of Quemado, New Mexico, and implement (A,b) was recovered from Tonque Pueblo (Barnett, 1969.104).

A **B**

Pot Support

Pot Support: These cooking jar or bowl supports, usually used in sets of three, were made from coarse clay. They do not seem to have been fired. It was probably not thought necessary because of their usual proximity to a fireplace or firepit in supporting a vessel during cooking. Note in view (A) the imprint of coiled basketry. Such imprints are also found on the opposite side and base. (B) is a side view.

Supports such as these were undoubtedly moved anywhere within a room to support a vessel, as well as over a fire (see Firedog). (Gladwin, *et al*, 1965.244 and Pl CCXII a & b.)

Pottery Smoothing Implement: These implements (sometimes called "**rubbing implements**"), were made from flat bone, potsherds, and pieces of gourd. They were used by potters to dress down the ropes of pottery material when a ceramic vessel was being shaped.

Implements of this kind are usually found associated with cultures which employed the coil rope method of making ceramic vessels (see Ceramic Making Tools).

B

C

Potsherd Pottery Smoothing Implements

Potsherd: These (B), like most artifacts made from potsherds, were well shaped by abrasion. They were, for the most part, shaped rectangular with rounded corners, oval, or in any shape convenient to the user. The implements were edge chipped to shape, and the edges of most were then abraded smooth. Some were drilled for wearing for handy use. Many are identified by a beveled edge, worn down from constant use.

94

Stone: This tool (C) (sometimes called a **"rubbing implement"**) was usually made from layered stone such as slate, schist, etc. The tool was often worked from a larger chip, and was tapered to a beveled or sharp edge. The flat sides are quite smooth, and often abraded. Length varies according to the size of the vessel on which it was used.

These items were used to smooth wet coils of clay in the shaping of ceramic vessels. They are also said to have been used for the removal of membranes and flesh from the fresh hides of animals (see Flesher).

Pounder: While these artifacts are identified as having been used as pounders (hammerstones or choppers), some were also used as grinding stones. The abraded sides with rounded corners, and ends which were convexed and scarred from pounding action, indicate their usage. Pieces of this kind were made from granite, basalt, or other hard stone, and weigh from 3.75 to 12.6 lbs each. They measure from 2⅞ to 7-13/16 inches (7.4 to 19.8 cm) long. Pounders were undoubtedly used to pulverize substances in a mortar, or to grind on any flat surface (also see Hammerstone and Pestle).

Squared pounders were only different because of their shape. Most pounders or pestles were cylindrically shaped. Square pounders were usually made from vesicular basalt and measure 2¼ inches (5.7 cm) long. The sides were concaved to form finger holds.

Pounding Stone, see Hammerstone

Prayer Stick: These were pieces of ornamental stone or wood (sometimes called a **"medicine cylinder," "paho,"** or **"medicine stick"**). Decorative stones such as honey onyx (A), banded calcite (B), hematite (C), or others were used. All were cylindrically shaped by abrasion. The lengths vary from 1¼ to over 3 inches (3.1 to over 7.5 cm) long.

Prayer sticks were also made from other kinds of stone, some of which were carved or graved. Those made from vesicular basalt (D,a)

each contain a deep narrow encircling groove near the rounded top. Some vesicular basalt sticks contain deviations from the so-called normal or single vertical prayer sticks. These would include the grooved sticks containing various degrees of curvature (D,b). Still another variation is (D,c). This piece contains a short projection, or a protrusion extending at an angle of approximately 25 degrees from the main stem of the stick. The short leg starts from just under the encircling groove near the top of the piece.

Thin encircling graved grooves are also found on the two basalt sticks (E). One of the more decorative sticks (F, front and side views), is a symbolic animal carved on the upper end of the piece.

One prayer stick (or *"paho"*) was recovered which had been carved cylindrically from a piece of cottonwood (G). The piece is 2-5/16 inches (5.87 cm) long by 1⅛ inches (2.85 cm) in diameter. It contains a bevel around both the top and bottom edges, and a 5/16 inch (0.79 cm) wide by 3/32 inch (0.24 cm) deep encircling groove just above the center of the piece.

The "sticks" were used much as the Zuni use modern wood prayer sticks today, *i.e.,* during a ceremonial, a feather or other streamer imbued with incantations was attached to the stick, and the combined piece then was stuck into the ground. The feather or streamer waved in the breeze, thus broadcasting the prayer far and wide.

Pounders

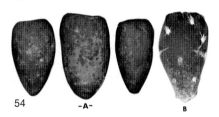

54   -A-   B

Reproductions of Pricklypear Cactus Fruit

Pricklypear Cactus Fruit, Reproduction of: The hand-molded reproductions of pricklypear cactus fruit (called **"tunas"**) (A), were made from a gray colored clay. Such reproductions are similar in size and shape to the actual fruit (B). The reproductions were painted a brown-red (probably hematite).

When ripe (purple to mahogany in color) the fruit was peeled and eaten by the Indians. Even today the ripe fruit is used to make jelly or candy.

As with the reproductions of the yucca seed pods, the cactus fruit reproductions are presumed to have been used symbolically during a

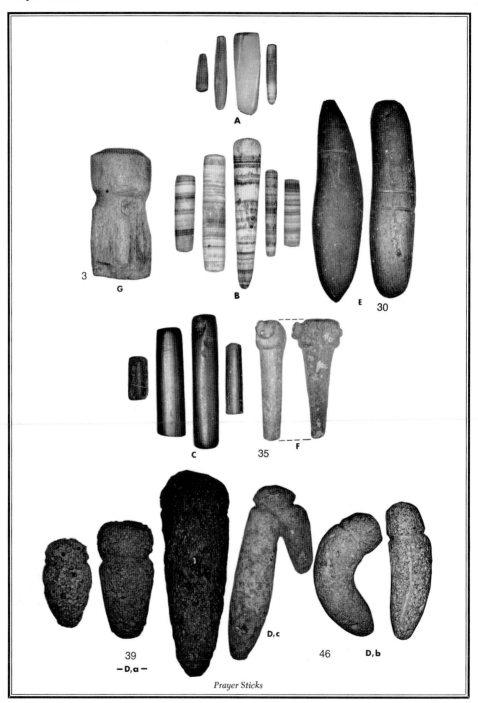

Prayer Sticks

ceremony, probably to induce larger future crops.

Projectile Point, see Arrowpoint or Spearpoint

Punch: While bone punches are not as plentiful as bone awls, nevertheless, they are found in fair quantity throughout ruins in the Southwest. These implements were made from small tubular bones of rodents. One or both joint ends were removed, and a sharp beveled or rounded

39

Bone Punches

point was worked on one end. The bevel-pointed end was used to cut out a hole in lightweight hides by punching. Many punches contain from one to three holes in the end opposite the beveled or worked end. These were probably used for stringing and wearing the tool for handy use.

Rabbit Net: The rabbit net is the largest game trap found to date. The net from White Dog Cave, Arizona, measures 240 feet (73.1 m) long by nearly 4 feet (1.2 m) wide. The meshes, made of a fiber string or cord, are approximately two inches (5.0 cm) square.

Such a net would be stretched across a narrow gorge, and a group of Indians, walking abreast, would beat the brush and drive whatever animals they were after into the net. The trapped animals were then shot with bows and arrows or spears, or were clubbed.

Rabbit Stick: Rabbit sticks (sometimes called **"throwing sticks [club],"** or **"fending sticks"**) are curved wooden sticks, some of which are as long as two feet (60.9 cm). Implements of this kind have been used by Indians of the South-

Rabbit Stick

west since Basketmaker times, and are still in use by the Zuni and Hopi of today.

It is thought that an early use might have been as a defensive fending stick — to strike away atlatl darts, or even a weapon in hand-to-hand combat. Sticks of this kind were used in communal rabbit hunts, as they are today. Many were carved with a series of grooves extending from the handle to the tip.

Rasp, Bone: This bone piece is presumed to be a rasp — a tool which was used to scrape or rub roughly, as with a coarse file. The implement was made from a large mammal tubular bone in which deep grooves were cut. It is also possible that the implement could have been used as a guiro (see Guiro).

1

Bone Rasp

Rasping Stick, see Guiro

Rattle, Deer Hoof: An instrument of this sort consisted of small groups of deer hooves, which were lashed together on a cord. When shaken together, they gave a hollow rattling sound.

Beside deer hooves, large sections of tubular mammal bones were also strung on separated cords, and when shaken together, they also gave off a hollow rattling sound (see Tinkler, Bone, or Pendant [Shell]).

This kind of rattle was undoubtedly used to

3

g

Deer Hoof Rattle

97

set the cadence of ceremonial or pleasure dances. A few instruments such as these have been recoverd from Basketmaker II caves in Arizona.

Rattle-Stone, Geode: When recovered from a Mimbres ruin in New Mexico, the geode had an opening which was closed by a wooden stopper. The geode contained over 20 small stones. When it was shaken rapidly, the stones gave out a sharp rattling sound (Nesbitt, 1931.87-89, Pl. 38).

WOOD STOPPER

5 **b**

Geode Rattle-Stone

Reamer: This tool (sometimes called a "**hand drill**") was used to taper or enlarge holes in bone, shell, ceramic material, and even stone. They were made from flint, agate, jasper, chert, obsidian, or other hard stone of local procurement. After a reamer was chipped to shape, it was often additionally sharpened by edge pressure retouch. Reamers are often identified by a large flange set at 90° to the shaft. This was for

Reamers

hand use of the tool. Many reamers were made from large arrowpoints or spearpoints which had become damaged and were subsequently reworked.

Most reamers contain a single point at one end and a flange at the other for grasping the instrument when in use. Many contain up to three points, each of a different shape or taper for various kinds of reaming jobs.

Reed Instrument, see Whistle, Bitsitsi

Reel, Pulley-Shaped: This pulley-shaped reel was hand-molded from clay, then fired. The piece measures 2-11/16 inches (1.74 cm) in diameter, and contains a deep groove encircling the periphery. There is some conjecture as to

the actual use or purpose of the reel, but it has been suggested that it might have been used to retain cotton cord, yucca fibers, and other similar use.

1
Pulley-Shaped Reel

Reel-Shaped Object: These hand-formed reel-shaped objects were made from clay, and, while smoothed and fired, were unpolished. (Gladwin, et al, 1965.243, Pl. CCXI a and c.) The two pieces pictured were recovered from the dump of a ruin south-south-east of Phoenix, Arizona. While

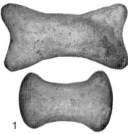
1
Reel-Shaped Objects

there is some question at to their actual use, it is thought that they were used as spools to retain cord, cotton yarn, or yucca fibers.

Resonator, see Bell (Copper), and Guiro

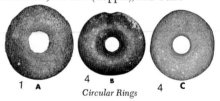
1 **A**   4 **B**   4 **C**
Circular Rings

Ring, Circular: The circular vesicular basalt (A), diorite (B), sandstone (C), or other local stone rings (sometimes called "**lava rings**" or "**doughnut-shaped digging-stick weights**"), measure approximately 3 inches (7.62 cm) outside diameter, and each contains a ⅝ to ⅞ inch (1.58 to 2.22 cm) diameter hole in the center. The pieces are quite symmetrical, and are abraded smooth. It is believed that items of this kind were used on the lower end of a planting stick as a "stop" to set a uniform depth for the planting of seeds.

Note the groove in the top of the diorite ring (B). It is assumed that the piece was utilized as a secondary shaft abrader.

Ring, Finger: Rings were small circular bands,

worn as personal adornment on a finger as they are today. They were made from bone, shell, and stone. Rings were made and worn by both men and women of all cultures of the Southwest.

Bone: Two general types of bone rings were found. The first, and more common, was made from a transverse-cut section of a large tubular mammal bone (A,a). Rings are usually carved, and abraded smooth. The one pictured (left) measures ½ inch (1.3 cm) inside diameter. Bone rings of this kind have been found which had been painted green and brown-red. The second one is consider-

Finger Rings

ably larger. It was found in the dump of a small ruin north of Quemado, New Mexico.

The second type, which is quite scarce, was made from the pelvic bone of a rabbit (A,b). The spongy bone around the oval hole has been abraded away, leaving a ¾ by ½ inch (1.8 by 1.3 cm) hole. This ring was excavated from a room at Fitzmaurice Pueblo Ruin (Barnett, 1973).

Shell: Some shell rings are actually smaller versions of bivalve shell bracelets (B,a), even

including the graving of geometrics. They were made in the same way, with the exception that they were cut considerably thinner. The umbo part was often abraded through, which made a hole for the additional use of wearing the piece in a necklace.

Another kind of shell ring was a section cut from a univalve shell (B,b). The side and edges were abraded quite smooth.

Stone: Stone rings (C) are considerably more scarce than either bone or shell, undoubtedly because of the difficulty in their fabrication. Usually a soft stone, such as argillite, was employed for this purpose. Some stone rings were graved with simple geometrics or crisscross motifs encircling them.

Ring, Lava, see Ring, Circular

Rock Carving, see Petroglyph

Roller, Weaving: Bone rollers, made from cylindrical sections of mammal bone, were cut

Bone Weaving Roller

to varying lengths. The ends were well abraded, as these rollers were used much as were battens — to separate warp threads during weaving operations. Many of these rollers were graved with simple geometrics, or encircling grooves.

Roof Beam Support, see Support Block

Rubbing Implement, see Pottery Smoothing Implement

Rubbing Stone, see Grinding Stone

Rubbing Tool, see Beaming Knife

S Saw : Scraper

Saw: These were cutting tools made from stone or bone. When made of stone, the small saws were generally similar to some edge scrapers, with the exception that a saw contained a series of sharp teeth notched into one edge. The teeth were generally spaced apart, though usually in line and not alternately deflected.

Bone: This unique bone saw (A) (damaged) was recovered from a ruin to the north of Quemado, New Mexico. It is a double-edged saw, being notched on both edges of the blade. The notches were abraded in the edges with a sharp abrading tool.

Stone: The small stone saws (B) were usually

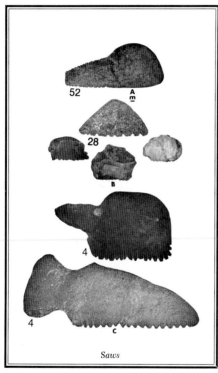

Saws

made from various sized chips of agate, chert, petrified wood, flint, or other local hard stone. They were used to cut sections of bone, wood, and shell.

The larger stone saws (C) were made with considerably more care than the smaller ones (B). Additionally, each large saw contains a handle. Note the pecking to shape of the groove between the handle and blade in the larger piece. Both of the larger implements are fine examples of prehistoric Indian craftsmanship.

Scapula, see Mammal Scapula, Decorated

Scepter, see Baton

Scoop, Sheep Horn: While this implement is presently called a "scoop," similar tools are sometimes referred to as "sickles." Actually the piece is an implement made from the horn of a young or female mountain sheep. The inside or core of the basal end has been removed, and the remaining edge abraded to a curved bevel.

The rounded edge suggests the usage of the implement as a scoop, as a flesher for the removal of flesh and fat from fresh hides, or as a "sickle" for cutting grasses or herbs. Artifacts of this kind were recovered from caves to the north of Navajo Mountain in Southern Utah.

3

Sheep Horn Scoop

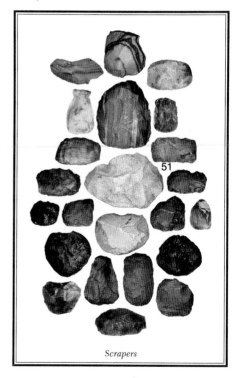

Scrapers

Scraper: These tools were made from flakes or chips of agate ,chert, schist, jasper, slate, obsidian, basalt, and many other kinds of stone, layered and otherwise. Many were chipped from larger chips, or were reworked fleshers or other similar tools. While many were worked to various shapes such as rectangular, oval, or square, others were merely chips sharpened by abrasion. Actually a scraper may be a mere chip or flake from a larger chunk of stone (see Chip and Core). However, a true scraper must show some evidence of having been man-worked (other than a particular shape), such as one or more chipped or flaked edges, or an edge showing wear by abrasion. Scrapers such as these have been given countless prefixes, depending upon their type or suggested or imaginary usage. Examples of such descriptive prefixes might be said to be: **"thumb scraper," "multiple scraper," "spokeshaver"** (bone or wood scraper with concaved edge), **"side scraper," "end scraper,"** and so on *ad infinitum*.

Large scrapers, made from slate, shale, rhyolite, and other similar stone, have also been used as knives and were sometimes edge-notched for hafting longitudinally at the thick edge opposite to the blade or sharpened edge. Such hafting consisted of a heavy twig which had been split lengthwise and located on the piece with half on each side. These pieces were bound securely on the short projecting

46

Scraper

ends with yucca cord. This addition to the stone piece provided a hand-hold for the user of the tool. It is said that large scrapers such as these were also used as mescal knives, although they were not serrated (notched) as were most mescal knives (see Mescal Knife).

Scrapers were used for cutting or scraping off membranous and fleshy material from fresh animal hides. These tools were also used as knives for working wood, bone, and shell implements, ornaments, etc. (see also Flesher).

Seed Beater: These objects (sometimes called **"beating sticks"**) were found in a granary of a cliffhouse in Northern Arizona. The beaters were made of five or six thin willow twigs, approximately 24 inches (61.0 cm) long, and secured together in line. The twigs were peeled,

except at the butts where they were fastened together with sinews and overwrapped with yucca cord (note detail of wrapped butt ends in photo). These beaters were undoubtedly used in the same manner as those used by Indians today — to knock various kinds of seeds into "sifters" (usually a flat basket affair), where they were tossed into the air so that the chaff was blown away and the seeds dropped back into the sifter.

HANDLE BINDING DETAIL

Seed Beaters

Set: A set is usually a small semiprecious gem stone or other ornamental stone which was abraded thin, then polished on the outer surface. They were usually made round, square, rectangular, or diamond shape, and were used as overlay or inlay on ornaments for personal adornment (see Color Plate I, Items 6 and 7, p. 10; and Overlay; and Inlay).

Shaft Abrader: A shaft abrader (sometimes called a **"shaft cleaner"**) was made from medium to coarse grain sandstone or vesicular basalt. Generally they were rough shaped square, rectangular,

39

12"=1'-0"=30.5 CM.

Shaft Abraders

101

or oval, and were grooved longitudinally. The upper surface (groove side) was flat, indicating that these abraders might have been used in matched pairs.

Because of the abrasive quality, such abraders were used to rough dress wood shafts of arrows and the shafts of bone items (awls, pins, battens, and spindles).

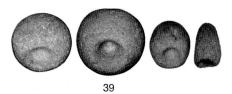

39

Shaft Holder

Shaft Holder: Shaft holders (sometimes called **"drill cups"**) were spherical or oval shaped stone pieces containing a single conical-shaped hole worked into one end to a depth of ¼ to ½ inch (0.6 to 1.25 cm). They were well smoothed and sized to be held comfortably in the cupped hand.

The holder was used to steady the upper end of the shaft of either a bow or pump drill when the tool was in use, and to permit the application of more pressure on the shaft for drilling.

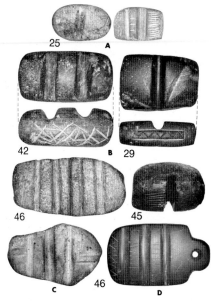

25   **A**

42   **B**   29

46   45

C   46   **D**

Shaft Polishers (I)

Shaft Polisher: These polishers, used on cylindrical wood and bone shaft-like items, worked a smooth polished finish after these items had been processed by rough abrasion. Polishers were made from various kinds of shaped hard stone such as granite, agate, basalt, soapstone, slate, argillite, and waterworn pebbles (A). Many polishers were shaped by pecking, and contain from one to five grooves. Most shaped polishers contain graved criss-cross or simple geometric motifs around the periphery (B).

39

12"=1'-0"=30.5 CM.

Shaft Polishers (II)

Some polishers contain what is termed a "T" groove (C). This consists of two grooves separated by a raised part, and that part set transversely to the main grooves of the polisher. The exact purpose of a polisher so designed is not as yet known.

A somewhat different shaft polisher is (D), which is not only made from argillite (an odd material for such usage), but also contains a drilled hole at one end, probably for suspension.

Polishers have been recovered which utilized large chunks of waterworn granite. These are considered more as fixed position polishers because of their size and weight, *i.e.*,

Passive Shaft Polisher

tools which were used from a certain position as opposed to an active portable, or hand operated item.

Shaft Scraper: This almost rectangular shaft scraper, made from vesicular basalt, was used

102

for much the same purpose as a shaft abrader (see Shaft Abrader), with the exception that the scraper was worked from the edge. The piece was used to rub off bark or small protrusions from wood shaft material, or to rough-dress shafts of bone which had been splintered from larger tubular bone.

Shaft Smoother: The shaft smoother was probably used after the shaft abrader and before the polisher. The piece generally contains a single groove, and was made from a stone

4

Shaft Scraper

containing a medium quality of abrasive. It was used to prepare a wood or bone shaft item for final polishing.

Shaft Straightener: Implements of this kind (sometimes called "wrenches") were usually made from antler, bone, or stone. A straightener contains one or two holes or notches, sometimes near one

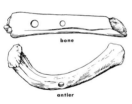

bone

antler

Shaft Straighteners

end, which were used as a lever for the straightening of a wood shaft piece. Such pieces probably were spindle shafts, foreshafts of arrows, pieces for cradle backs, and many other wood shaft-like pieces which required straightening. These were probably soaked in water or steamed to make them pliable prior to using the straightener. (Kidder, 1932.240-241 and Fig. 201; and Martin, *et al*, 1961.89 and Fig. 63.)

Shuttle: The short implements pictured in the Weaving Tools illustration are assumed to be shuttles — implements used to carry ends of thread back and forth during weaving operations. It is suggested that different colors of weaving materials were attached to the piece, and the tool passed back and forth, probably over the batten. Shuttles were made of bone or wood.

Sickle, see Scoop, Sheep Horn

Shaft Smoother : Sipapu

39

Sinkers

Sinker: As the name implies, these were weights used in fishing. They were usually small flat waterworn stones of any kind, in which a small hole had been perforated near one end. They have been recovered in a number of places in the Southwest near water — lakes, streams, rivers.

Sinker, Net: This vesicular basalt object is elliptical-shaped and measures 6-1/16 inches (15.2 cm)long by 4 inches (10.16 cm) wide, by 1¾ inches (4.44 cm) thick. It contains a

49

Net Sinker

9/16 inch (1.43 cm) wide by 5/16 inch (0.79 cm) deep encircling longitudinal groove. It weighs 1.31 lbs.

Net sinkers were used as fishing net sinkers or weights on the lower edge of a vertical seine when the net was stretched across a creek or channel to catch fish. This particular net sinker was recovered in north-central Arizona.

Sipapu: The two items pictured consist of a sipapu cover (A) and a sipapu (B). These pieces were recovered from a kiva

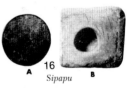

A   16   B

Sipapu

ruin near Zuni, New Mexico. The sipapu was a symbolic sacred hole of emergence, usually found embedded in the center of the floor in a ceremonial chamber of a kiva. The sipapu pictured was worked from a large block of sandstone. The circular opening is larger at the lower end than the upper — almost funnel-shaped. The smaller diameter orifice was located at the top (floor level), and the lower, which was larger, contains a through hole. The circular disc, which forms the cover for the sipapu opening, was made from a well-rounded and abraded piece of gray slate. Many variations of sipapus are found (usually in kivas of pueblo ruins) in the American Southwest, though few are removable because of their construction.

Skinning Knife : Snare

Skinning Knife: This thin-bladed black slate utensil was used as an aid in stripping skins from freshly-killed animals. It was abraded quite smooth, and has a sharp tapered cutting edge. The knife measures 6 inches (15.24 cm) long. A hole was started at the upper end of the handle, but was not drilled through the piece. This skinning knife is of Hohokam origin.

46

Skinning Knife

Slab Metate, see Metate, Type V, Flat-Thin

Smoke Blower, see Pipe

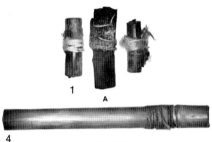

Smoking Tubes

Smoking Tube: Smoking tubes (generally referred to as **"cigarettes"**) consist of sections of *Phragmites communis* or *P. phragmites* species of reed cane, in which varying amounts of species of the genus *Nicotiana attenuata* (a prehistoric "tobacco") were smoked ceremonially in the Southwest (Switzer, 1969.49-51). Thus the tube was reused as desired. Based upon the actual use of the smoking tubes, the term "cigarette" for this artifact is somewhat of a misnomer. Based upon definition, a cigarette is tobacco wrapped and smoked within a cylinder of thin paper, corn husk, or other papery material, during which both are consumed.

An undecorated smoking tube is one which does not contain a wrapping of any sort. All of those pictured are considered as "decorated" (wrapped). Three are wrapped with yarn or yucca fiber, while the fourth (A) is woven cotton, sash-wrapped and bound in place with yarn.

Smoother, see Floor Smoother, and Shaft Smoother

Smoothing Stone, see Polishing Stone

Snare: This was a trapping device used to catch birds and small rodents such as squirrels, rabbits, rats, gophers, prairie dogs, and field mice. There were three major types used: the single-cord slip-noose, a net which was encircled by a noose, and bird snare sticks.

Slip-Noose: The slip-noose was usually made from a cord of human hair or fibers from yucca leaves. One end of the cord was passed through a loop on the far end, and secured to a low bent tree branch or a peg in the ground (see Snare Pin, Bone). The noose was set in a circle in which bait of one sort or another had been placed. The bird or rodent would trip the loop and be caught in the noose, which would tighten.

Net: The net with the encircling noose worked in much the same way as the single-cord slip-noose except that the net was more often spread over a burrow or in a runway frequented by various kinds of rodents. The net would enmash the animal in either event.

Stick Snare: One of the more ingenious bird snares is the "stick" snare. These were made from nearly straight unpeeled sticks which ranged from 9¾ to 24⅝ inches (47.5 to 64 cm) long, by 7/32 to 5/16 inch (0.5 to 0.8 cm) in diameter. Each stick has from two to six short lengths of human hair cord attached at intervals along its length. These are secured to the  stick at intervals of 1⅝ to 2⅜ inches (4.0 to 6.0 cm) apart with yucca fibers, except for one where sinew was used. When in use, the stick was buried shallowly in the ground and cornmeal or other similar bait was spread around the area of the series of loops at the ends of the cords. The hair slips easily and entraps the bird. However, none of the sticks were recovered with attached loops (Lindsay, *et al*, 1968.67-69). These bird stick snares

Stick Snares

were recovered from a cave near Navajo Mountain, in Southern Utah.

Snare Pin, Bone: This pin was used to secure one end of a slip-noose snare to the ground (see Snare, Slip-Noose). The pin pictured was made from a piece of bone which measures 1-25/32 inches (4.5 cm) long by 15/32 inch (1.1 cm) wide by 7/32 (0.5 cm) thick. It was secured to the net by yucca fibers. Snare pins are usually found in caves along with the snares.

3
9

Bone
Snare Pin

Sounding Rasp, see Guiro

Spear: This instrument (also called a **"lance"**) is a thrusting or throwing weapon used during close fighting or the hunt. It consists of a long wooden shaft with a large stone spear-point firmly attached to one end. The length seems to have been a matter of choice of the user, though they were usually longer than the height of the warrior. Those spears which have been found in the Southwest have been in caves.

Spearpoint: A spearpoint (sometimes called a **"projectile point"**) may generally be considered an enlarged version of an arrowpoint. They were made from the same materials and in a similar manner (see Arrowpoints). Spearpoints were large heavy points attached to long wooden shafts (spear), and used as weapons either during the hunt or in combat.

Spearpoints

Spear Sling, see Atlatl

Spear Thrower, see Atlatl

Spear-Thrower Weight, see Atlatl Weight

Sphere, Stone, see Ball, Stone

Spindle Shaft Holder: A spindle shaft holder or base consists of a hole in an otherwise unworked stone, or a metate or mano fragment. The piece, made from any kind of stone, was placed on the ground (or floor). It held the

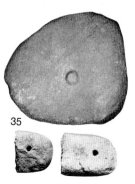

35

Spindle Shaft Holders

lower end of the spindle shaft while the fibers were being twisted into thread (see Hand Spinning illustration, also Shaft Holder). These artifacts were widely used in the American Southwest.

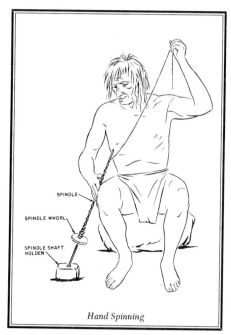

SPINDLE

SPINDLE WHORL

SPINDLE SHAFT HOLDER

Hand Spinning

Spindle Whorl: These artifacts were used as balance wheels (sometimes called **"balance discs"**) on spindles when fibers were being hand spun into cords for later weaving operations (see "Spindle Shaft Holder"). They were made from worked potsherds, from discoidal stones, or from hand-molded clay material.

105

Splitter : Split-Twig Fetish

Spindle whorls or balance discs (generally of the discoidal kind) were also used as flywheels on the shafts of pump and bow drills during

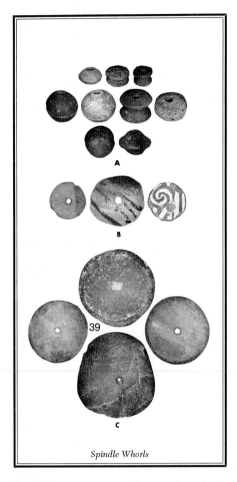

Spindle Whorls

the drilling operation. The weight of the spindle whorl would aid in the uniformity of the clockwise and counterclockwise rotary motion of the shafts.

Clay Material: The spool- or pulley-shaped whorls (A) (Haury, 1945.115-118), were as crudely hand-molded as fetishes and figurines. They are generally round and contain a groove encircling the periphery. There is a hole near the center which secured the whorl to the spindle. Spindle whorls measure from 25/32 to 1½ inches (1.9 to 3.7 cm) in diameter by 9/16 to 1 inch (1.4 to 2.5 cm) thick. They weigh from 0.015 to 0.078 lb.

Holes such as those found in hand-molded spindle whorls, were made by forcing a twig of the desired diameter through the center of the spindle whorl; then when the piece was fired, the twig was burned out, leaving the hole.

Potsherd: These were disc-shaped pieces made from potsherds (B). A hole for the spindle is in the center of the piece. The edges of most pieces were abraded smooth, but the circularity is quite variable, ranging from near perfect circles to sub-quadrate forms. This condition also applies to those spindle whorls made from stone. These perforated discs are found throughout the Southwest. They generally measure up to 2 inches (5.0 cm) in diameter.

Stone: While spindle whorls made from stone (C) are not as common as those made from ceramic material or potsherds, they have been recovered from most areas of the Southwest. They were made from any kind of layered stone, and from discoidal-shaped waterworn stones. All were perforated, generally in the center, with a single hole. Such pieces were abraded smooth on both sides and around the peripheral edge.

Splitters

Splitter: These heavy, crude, maul-like tools were used to split wood (logs), or to separate layered-type stone. They were chipped roughly to the shape of a single-bladed axe, with the exception of the narrow blade. They contain a rounded shaped poll. Of those pictured, one was edge grooved and the other was full grooved for hafting. Splitters weigh from 4.5 to 6.0 lbs each, and are made from any kind of stone. They measure approximately 13 inches (33.0 cm) long by 7½ to 8¼ inches (19.0 to 20.95 cm) wide by 2 to 2¼ inches (5.08 to 5.71 cm) thick. They have been found in widely separated areas in the Southwest.

Split-Twig Fetish: These unique artifacts, which have been dated as over 4,000 years old, were recovered from both the Grand and Marble Canyons, in Arizona. Each of the many

3

Split-Twig Fetish

1

Spoon-Shaped Dipper

south-southeast of Phoenix, Arizona. The piece measures 6-7/16 inches (16.4 cm) long. The only embellishment is a rather shallow groove on top of the handle and extending its full length.

Staff, see Baton

minor variations of the fetish pictured was made from single green willow twigs which had been partially split, then worked into the kind of animal fetish shown.

These fetishes are said to have been secreted behind or between rocks located in or near caves which were frequented by deer, antelope, or other animals searching for water or rest. These fetishes were supposed to have been for the purpose of inducing more animals into the caves, where they were hunted down by the Indians.

Spokeshave Scraper, see Scraper (with concaved edge)

Spoon, Antler: This piece, almost like a scoop, was made from the joint of an antler. The prongs have been removed, and the piece has been abraded so that the center portion of the "inverted Y" is deep, and the entire piece is quite smooth. It was undoubtedly used to spoon meal from a container to a cooking vessel, or

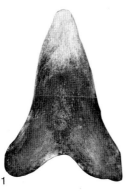

1

Antler Spoon

vice versa. This antler spoon was recovered from a cave.

Spoon-Shaped Dipper: This utility implement was beautifully made from a fine grade of schist like a modern-day spoon.

It was recovered from a prehistoric ruin

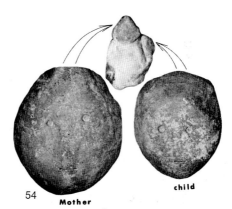

54   **Mother**   **child**

Effigy Statue

Statue, Effigy: Sculptured stone images (also called "full figure images") of this kind are extremely rare in the Southwest. The one pictured was recovered from Tonque Pueblo Ruin, north of Albuquerque, New Mexico. The piece, crudely worked of sandstone, stands 10¼ inches (26.0 cm) high, and weighs 12 lbs. The piece depicts a Mother holding a child in her left arm. The faces of each, detailed in the enlargements, were painted a brown-red (probably hematite). With the exception of the few features consisting of slight raises for noses, shallow drilled or reamed holes for eyes, and thin grooves for mouths, the faces are otherwise quite flat. Statues of this kind were usually made for ceremonial purposes.

Stone images recovered from the Pecos Pueblo Ruin (1915 and 1925) are among the very few such artifacts of this nature found in the Southwest (Kidder, 1932.88-91). The one found at Tonque Pueblo Ruin (pictured) com-

107

pares favorably in workmanship with those from Pecos.

Reminiscent of such full-figure images might also be those found at Snaketown (Sacaton Phase) (Gladwin, *et al*, 1965. Plate CXCVI). These were made of hand-molded clay and decorated, and were found in cremations. They compare with those recovered from the Casas Grandes Ruin in Mexico.

Stone Cylinder, see Cylinder, Vesicular Basalt, Small

Stone Image, see Statue, Effigy

Stopper, Clay, see Pot Stopper

Support Block: These

Support Blocks

heavy pieces (sometimes called **"roof beam supports"**) were chipped and/or pecked to square shapes from large chunks of granite, rhyolite, or other local hard stone. Because of their very nature, these blocks are considered to have been used as supports for roof beams, or other construction purposes. Regardless of the shape or the method of shaping, the size variation, both in thickness and length, is considerable.

Chipped: Supports were shaped by chipping from any kind of rock. Some were shaped generally round, while others were roughly square. They generally measure from 3⅜ to 7 by as much as 44 inches long (9.2 to 17.7 by 111.8 cm). Supports have been found weighing as much as 103 lbs.

Pecked: Supports which were pecked to shape and those that were shaped by chipping are similar in measurements and weights.

Throwing Stick (Club), see Rabbit Stick, or Atlatl

Tinkler, Bone: This bone piece was one of many, generally worn in series on the arms, legs, waist, or across the chest during a dance, usually of a ceremonial nature. A series, or several series of these tinklers give a pleasing short light clinking sound when rattled together.

The piece pictured is from a large bird bone from which both joint ends have been removed. The shaft was highly polished and the ends were rounded. A thin strip of rawhide was passed through a perforation in the upper end and used for attaching the piece to groups of others. (see Rattle, Deer Hoof or Pendant [Shell]). This particular tinkler

3

Bone Tinkler

was found in a cave in Northern Arizona. Tinklers have been recovered by excavation but with the rawhide rotted away.

Tomahawk, see Axe

Tong: These large tongs (sometimes called **"fire tongs"**), made from a yucca fruit stem bent double in the middle, was a device used for the ease or convenience of handling or lifting hot items (as from a fire). Note that both of the extension ends were burned from such use. The extension arms each measure approximately 12⅞ to 13 inches (32.71 to 33.02 cm) in length. This item was recovered from a cave in east-central Arizona.

Tooma, see Cooking Slab

53

Tongs

Torch: This piece consists of a bundle of strips of juniper bark, which was bound securely with five separate wraps of yucca fibers. While this item is identified as a "torch," it is suggested that it may possibly have served as a brush. This torch was found in a cave in Southern Arizona.

Torch, Juniper-Bark: These strips of juniper bark are identified as torches, and are said to have been used in the "Fire Ceremony" to carry fire and light from one room to another. These pieces were recovered from the floor of a ruin in Northern New Mexico (Judd, 1954.278 and Pl. 79).

1

Torch

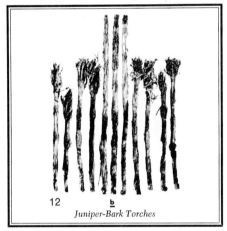

12

Juniper-Bark Torches

Toy (?): This piece was made from two flat split twigs, which were folded back and forth at right angles to each other.

The crossed twigs were secured vertically by a heavier split twig, the protruding pieces of which were bound by being wrapped with a piece of split twig.

3

Toy (?)

The piece was found in a cave to the northeast of Navajo Mountain in Southern Utah, and

is said to be a toy which had been hung from the hood of a child's cradle board. However, it is also possible that the item could have been ceremonially used — indicating the four directions (north, south, east, and west). Four-way charms indicating the four directions have been recovered which were made of stone, shell, and bone.

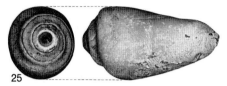

25

Trumpet

Trumpet: This large univalve shell (*Strombus galeatus*) was made into a trumpet by the simple expedient of abrading the apex of the spire away, and smoothing the remaining round opening. Trumpets like the one pictured from the Tonto Basin area in Arizona have been recovered in a number of ruins in the Southwest.

By compressing the lips and blowing into the spire end, one can produce a deep penetrating tone which can be heard from a long distance. It is believed that a trumpet of this kind would be ceremonially used, rather than as a musical instrument.

Tunas, see Pricklypear Cactus Fruit, Reproduction of

Turkey Call, see Whistle (Bone)

Unperforated Disc, see Disc, Plain

109

Vessel, Miniature:
Miniature vessels were used as containers for discoidal beads, small seeds, or other such items.
Stone: Small stone vessels were usually well made from easily worked stone by pecking to shape, then fine abrasion (A,a). The rectangular vessel pictured was made from a red vesicular limestone, and was smooth finished both inside and outside.

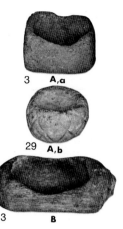

3   **A,a**

29   **A,b**

3   **B**

Miniature Vessels

The small round vessel (A,b) was made from a piece of gray indurated sandstone. It was decorated with a simple encircling series of graved diamond cross-hachured lines.
Wood: This small vessel, carved from cottonwood, has been termed a dipper, scoop, and other names — some appropriate, and others not. The piece was well made, and *could* have had a handle (much like a dipper). The cross grain of the end shows rough, but this is not considered sufficient evidence of once having had a handle. However, regardless of the various suppositions, the piece is a miniature wood vessel, which was recovered from a cave in Northern Arizona.

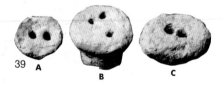

39   **A**

B

C

Wall Plugs

Wall Plug: These unfired clay pieces are usually recovered from ruins of pueblo-type dwellings. They were used as plugs in holes or vents in interior or exterior walls, either to cut down or admit ventilation or drafts. Additionally, they were used to plug holes into the vertical ventilator shafts.

Most plugs were hand-shaped much like a truncated cone; however, some have a base similar to a heavy-stemmed mushroom. Dimensions across the head measure, generally, 5 by 7 to 6 inches (12.7 by 17.7 to 15.2 cm) and bases vary between 3½ and 4-1/16 inches (8.9 and 10.2 cm). The head of each plug contains either two or three finger holes (for insertion

into or removal from the vent), which are smooth and range from ½ to ⅝ inch (1.3 to 1.6 cm) in diameter to 1½ inches (3.8 cm) deep. The plugs weigh from 1.3 to 5.4 lbs each.

Plug (A) was recovered from Tonque Pueblo (Barnett, 1969.137). Plug (B) was recovered from a site east of Albuquerque, New Mexico, and plug (C) was recovered from a site to the northwest of Albuquerque, New Mexico.

Wall Polisher, see Floor Smoother

Wall Smoother, see Floor Smoother

Wand: Both of the wands pictured are slightly damaged (though [B] is more so). These pieces were beautifully graved on a polished shaft of a large mammal tubular bone. A staff of this sort was usually carried as a symbol of authority, or as a rod supposedly containing magical power for the possessor. Wand (A) was recovered from a burial west of Tonto Basin, Arizona, and wand (B) from a burial in northeastern Arizona.

Weaving Fork, see Comb, Weaving

Weaving Pin: These "pins" were made in varying lengths and, like a weaving comb, were used to beat down the weft in place during weaving on a vertical loom. Such pins were made from bone, mesquite, or wood.

Bone: This series of bone tools was originally made for use as awls. However, because of their weight or size, they were also used as an implement to beat down the weft during weaving. These tools may be identified by the one or more highly polished diagonal grooves located along the shaft of the tool.

Mesquite: This 9½ inches (24.1 cm) long tool made from a straight piece of mesquite was found in a cave in the Verde Valley. Part of

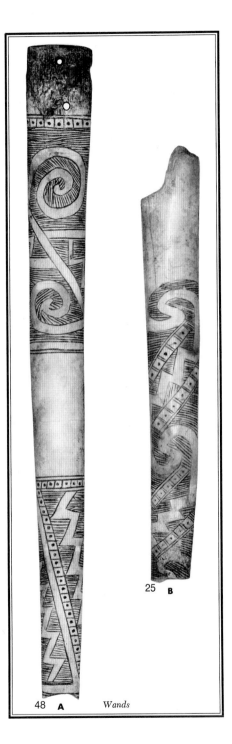

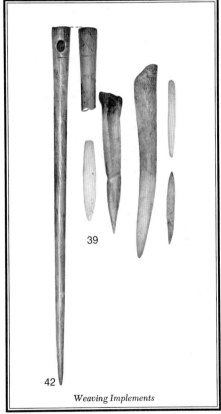

Weaving Implements

the inside fibers were removed, and the tool was abraded smooth and beautifully polished on the outside. A hole was drilled through one wall near the large end, probably for attaching the piece to a thong to insure easy accessibility when weaving. The large end contains graved simple criss-cross geometric

Wands

111

Weaving Tool : Whistle

decoration on the side opposite to that containing the hole.

Weaving Tool: Tools used in various weaving operations were made from antler, bone, mesquite, and wood. Some of these tools were re-used bone awls. Undoubtedly there were additional tools which were made from wood, but, except for those recovered from dry caves, these would have disintegrated by action of earth-damp over the centuries.

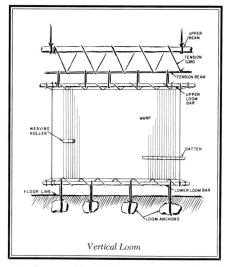

Vertical Loom

Implements identified as weaving tools and generally used with a vertical loom are found under the following headings:

Batten
Comb, Weaving
Hair Ornament
Roller, Weaving
Shuttle
Weaving Pin

Wedge: These implements, somewhat similar in shape to firedogs, were usually shaped by chipping from almost any kind of easily worked stone. They are similar in shape to a modern-day wedge, and were undoubtedly used for much the same purpose. Most wedges average approximately 6 to 7 inches (15.2 to 17.7 cm) long. The wedge pictured (front and side views) was made from slate.

Wedge

Weight, Doughnut-Shaped Digging-Stick, see Ring, Circular

Whetstone, see Abrading Stone

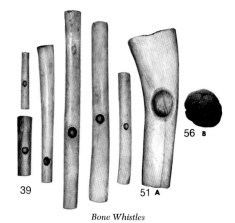

Bone Whistles

Whistle: Whistles were used as musical wind instruments during ceremonials. Regardless of kind, they emit a shrill high-pitched sound. They were also used by hunters for attracting birds, or even certain mammals. When one used the single hole cylindrical bone whistle, the whistling sound was produced by holding the thumb and index finger over opposite ends of the bone while blowing across the hole.

Bone: Whistles (the smaller ones are sometimes called "turkey calls," or "bird-calls") were made from sections of shafts of varying lengths of tubular bones from rodents and large birds. The joint ends of the bones were removed and the remaining 5/16 to ½ inch (0.8 to 1.2 cm) diameter shaft was sectioned into 1¾ to 5-11/16 inches (4.4 to 14.5 cm) lengths, as desired. A single stop-hole was drilled or reamed in one side near one end, or in the middle of the shaft. Some of these instruments were graved with simple geometrics, and many were polished.

Probably one of the largest whistles recovered is item (A) in the figure. It measures 4½ inches (11.4 cm) long with a 1½ to 15/16 inch (3.8 to 2.4 cm) oval opening at one end and a ⅞ inch (2.2 cm) diameter opening at the other. The stop-hole measures ¾ inch (1.9 cm) and was reamed or abraded at a bevel to a ½ inch (1.3 cm) diameter opening. The piece was cut from a large (approximately 5/32 inch (0.3 cm) thick walled section of mammal bone. The inside surface at each end had been abraded, forming a semi-sharp edge. This whistle was recovered from a ruin in Middle Verde, west of Camp Verde, Arizona.

Stone: The generally spherical-shaped stone whistle pictured (B) was made from a small hollow chunk of a lime-chert concretion. The piece has been partially abraded to remove rough surface projections. The hole appears to have been reamed. This whistle was found in a ruin located to the north of Quemado, New Mexico.

Whistle, Bitsitsi: Construction of the bitsitsi

whistle (reed instrument), includes two small rectangular-shaped pieces cut from large thin-walled bones (probably tubular bird bone). The longitudinal sides of the bone were abraded in such a manner that when the two pieces were placed together, the sides matched. A vibrator, such as a thin piece of gut or a blade of grass, was placed between the two pieces and the parts then bound together, forming the whistle (Hodge, 1920.130-131; and Webb, 1961). The instrument emits a shrill raucous sound when blown into.

Bitsitsi Whistle

Wrench, see Shaft Straightener

Yucca Seed Pod, Reproduction of:
The two reproductions of the yucca seed pods (A) were made from a red clay containing small "rice" size gravel. The reproductions are of much the same size and shape as the growing, or real, pod (B). They were painted a grass-green color.

54   -A-   B

Reproductions of Yucca Seed Pod

The yucca, a plant of the lily family native to the Southwest, furnished food and craft material for the prehistoric Indian. The seeds found in the pod were dried and roasted for food.

The fibers from the long leaves were used to make twine, brushes, matting, and basketry.

The reproductions are presumed to have been used, symbolically, in a ceremony held for the purpose of producing larger crops. These, along with the Pricklypear Cactus reproductions noted elsewhere in this Dictionary, were found in northwest New Mexico.

ARTIFACTS
OF UNKNOWN USAGE

This seemingly odd category, which might also be called "unknown miscellany," is included to cover those few artifacts whose use is not known, but which are often described as "problematical," "miscellaneous," "ceremonial," "unknown object," and so on *ad infinitum* in various archaeological publications. In general, these artifacts are those which do not conform to any present-day known usage, purpose, or even category. Often seemingly odd items were made by individual Indians for some specific purpose. Among others, the Hohokam are notorious for producing quantities of such items whose usage is presently unidentifiable.

The following information consists of purely descriptive matter, and no attempt is made to embellish a given piece. The items are pictured as an aid to possible identification.

The capital letter preceding each descriptive paragraph corresponds to that letter below the photograph of the item in the figure.

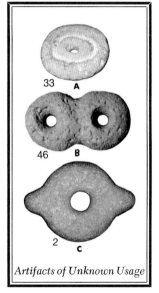

Artifacts of Unknown Usage

A. This disc-like piece of vesicular basalt measures 6⅝ inches (16.58 cm) in diameter by 1-⅝ inches (4.13 cm) thick. The hole in the center was drilled or reamed through. The center phase is slightly raised, as is the outer phase. The groove encircles the piece on top. The bottom is flat, and the entire disc has been abraded quite smooth.

B. The figure "8" double-doughnut-shaped piece was made from vesicular basalt. The piece measures 10 inches (25.4 cm) across, with each ring being 5¼ inches (13.3 cm) in diameter by approximately 2⅛ inches (5.4 cm) thick. Note that each hole contains an encircling biconical shape, indicating possible use as a shaft smoother, or from having been so reamed.

C. An odd sandstone artifact is the doughnut-shaped piece containing small balanced protrusions on each side, opposite to each other. The piece measures 1½ inches (3.81 cm) outside diameter by 9/16 inch (1.42 cm) thick. The rounded protrusions each extend 5/16 inch (0.79 cm) beyond the exterior diameter of the piece.

GLOSSARY

These are definitions and/or explanations of terms as used in, and applied to this Dictionary.

Aborigine: The native inhabitant; in the Southwest, the early Indian.

Active Artifact: An artifact where the energy is hand-activated; portable (*i.e.*, shaft polisher, polishing stone, abrader, grinding stone, etc).

Archaeology: The recovery and study of the material culture or remains, of human life and activities relating to prehistoric peoples.

Artifact: An article of human workmanship. A term applied to the implements, tools, weapons, charms and ornaments, and ceremonial objects as used in this instance by the prehistoric Indians.

Bivalve: A mollusk (such as an oyster, clam, etc) consisting of two halves (valves), which, hinged together, form the complete shell.

Campsite: A temporary camp area, usually near water, which was frequented by nomadic Indians, hunters, harvesters of mesquite beans and other wild seeds, cactus fruit, and berries. A stone quarry.

Ceramic (Pottery) Material: Usually a fine grade of argil (clay), with temper added, used to fashion ceramic vessels.

Clay: Any type of clay (with or without inclusions) generally used for the making of ceramic vessels, figurines, fetishes, some ornaments and charms, etc.

Culture: The possessions, geographic location, and the pattern of life of a group of Indians which differentiated them from another.

Dress: To make straight, or shape by removal of rough areas. To smooth and polish.

Dump: A rubbish pile, usually adjacent to or nearby a prehistoric Indian pueblo or other dwelling, or a campsite. An area where they unloaded their house trash, sometimes referred to as a "midden."

Earth-Damp: A condition of the soil which retains and maintains natural dampness. It is found at varying depths (though generally greater) from the surface of the earth, depending upon regional climatic conditions and the resultant evaporation, as well as the composition of the soil itself. This condition as opposed to soil immediately dampened to lesser depths by atmospheric moisture such as rain, snow, fog, etc. The earth-damp condi-

117

tion causes a chemical action which in turn causes decomposition of bone, cloth, wood, metal, etc.

Face: The worked surface portion of an artifact. To put on a smooth surface.

Fieldstone: Stone as taken from the field. Natural stone, unworked.

Geometric Shapes: Characterized by external outline, or regular forms composed of curves, angles, or straight line (*i.e.*, circle, square, rectangle, pear-shape, triangle, or a composite of phases of these).

Grave(d): To carve out or incise, as with a sharp tool.

Haft (Hafted): That part of a weapon or other implement which is made with a partial or completely encircling groove in which a handle, sling, or similar attachment may be fitted.

Hard and Tough: This term, applied to stone, indicates that kind of material which contains, fully, the multiple properties of "hard" — solid and compact, and "tough" — cohesive.

Igneous: Applies to the highly compressed condition of rock which is formed by the solidification of volcanic action or intense heat.

Indurated: Hardened — highly compacted.

Kiva: A ceremonial council chamber, and often a "lounging room" for men. Such a room, generally round though sometimes rectangular, usually contained an altar (which was changed according to the clan using the chamber), and sometimes a sipapu. Light was generally admitted from a hole in the center of the roof, which with the aid of a ladder, was also used as an entrance and exit.

Lithic: Made from any kind of stone.

Longitudinal Axis: Extending lengthwise, around which the parts of a thing are arranged .

Motif: Generally infers a specific part or phase of decoration.

Passive Artifact: Generally a utility-type item, often in a natural fixed position. Not portable.

Peck(ed): To strike a stone with a hard pointed or rough stone. To shape a piece of stone by removal of small bits of stone by striking (pecking) with another. To mark a stone by pecking.

Pit-House: A prehistoric Indian dwelling dug in the ground and roofed over with tree limbs, branches, and mud. The entrance, which was tunneled into one end, sometimes also acted as a smoke vent.

Pit(ted): To mark or roughen a smooth surface with minute depressions or chips (as on a mano or metate for a better grinding surface). To peck as with a hammerstone or pounder (see Peck[ed]).

Point(ed): The distinguishing feature of the tapering sharp or projecting end of an artifact (*i.e.*, bone or wood awl, needle, hair ornament, pin, etc).

118

Poll: The flat, blunt, or rounded end of a tool (such as an axe). That part at the opposite end from the blade edge.

Potsherd: A fragment of an item of ceramic ware (usually from a vessel).

Prehistoric: Of, or happening in, a time prior to recorded history or the coming of the Spanish into the Southwest (A.D. 1540).

Pueblo: A kind of communal Indian village in the Southwest, named "pueblo" by the invading Spanish. In prehistoric times, most such villages consisted of a series of connected or contiguous masonry or mud-walled rooms, usually of one floor, though sometimes having two or more.

Sherd: A fragment or segment (also called "shard," which is the European version) of a piece of pottery (ceramic ware) — a potsherd — from which certain secondary artifacts are sometimes made, *i.e.*, spindle whorl, disc (perforated or unperforated), pendant, jar cover, gaming piece, etc.

Site: The location of an area occupied by prehistoric Indians in a house, a group of houses, or town (pueblo). Additionally a temporary stopping place such as a quarry, harvesting area, summer farm field, etc.

Transverse: Crossing from side to side — placed across.

Univalve: A mollusk (gastropod sea shell) having but a single shell.

Worked Surface: A specific surface for a given use or purpose which is formed as the result of man's efforts. This is distinct from a natural surface created by phenomena such as water flow, weather conditions (heat and cold), slide, etc.

ADDITIONAL
REFERENCE MATERIAL

This section of selected reference material is included for the benefit of the student who desires further detail, or comparative material, concerning a given artifact or series thereof.

GENERAL SOUTHWEST

AMSDEN, CHARLES A.

    1949   *Prehistoric Southwesterners from Basketmaker to Pueblo.* Los Angeles Southwest Museum, Los Angeles, California

CUMMINGS, BYRON

    1953   *First Inhabitants of Arizona and the Southwest.* Cummings Publication Council, Tucson, Arizona

GLADWIN, HAROLD S.

    1957   *A History of the Ancient Southwest.* The Bond Wheelwright Co., Portland, Maine

HEWETT, EDGAR L.

    1948   *Ancient Life in the American Southwest.* Tudor Publishing Co., New York

KIDDER, ALFRED V.

    1962   *An Introduction to the Study of Southwestern Archaeology.* Yale University Press, New Haven and London

WORMINGTON, H. M.

    1957   *Ancient Man in North America.* The Denver Museum of Natural History, Denver, Colorado

TEXT REFERENCE MATERIAL

ABBOTT, R. TUCKER

    1961   *How to Know the American Marine Shells.* The New American Library of World Literature, Inc., New York

    1962   *Sea Shells of the World.* Golden Press, New York

BARNETT, FRANKLIN

    1969   *Tonque Pueblo — A Report of Partial Excavation of an Ancient Pueblo*

IV Indian Ruin in New Mexico. The Albuquerque Archaeological Society, Albuquerque, New Mexico

1970 *Matli Ranch Ruins — A Report of Excavation of Five Small Prehistoric Indian Ruins of the Prescott Culture in Arizona.* Technical Series No. 10, Northern Arizona Society of Science and Art, Inc., Flagstaff, Arizona

1973 *Excavation of Main Pueblo at Fitzmaurice Ruin — Prescott Culture in Yavapai County, Arizona.* (In Press)

COLTON, HAROLD S.

1960 *Black Sand — Prehistory in Northern Arizona.* p. 65 (ball, rubber); and pp. 44–45, 49, 65 (ball courts). University of New Mexico Press, Albuquerque, New Mexico

CUSHING, FRANK H.

1966 *Zuni Fetishes.* K. C. Publications, Flagstaff, Arizona

DUTTON, BERTHA P.

1963 *Sun Father's Way — The Kiva Murals of Kuaua.* The University of New Mexico Press, Albuquerque, New Mexico; The School of American Research, Santa Fe, New Mexico; and The Museum of New Mexico Press, Santa Fe, New Mexico

GLADWIN, HAROLD S.; HAURY, EMIL W.; SAYLES, E. B.; and GLADWIN, NORA

1965 *Excavations at Snaketown — Material Culture*; pp. 233–245; p. 243, and Pl. CCXI a, b, and c; p. 244, and Pl. CCXII a and b; pp. 163–165, 278–281 (copper bells); and p. 48 (Haury) (ball, rubber); and pp. 36–49 (Haury) (ball courts). The University of Arizona Press, Tucson, Arizona

HAURY, EMIL W.

1945 *The Excavation of Los Muertos and Neighboring Ruins in the Salt River Valley, Southern Arizona.* Peabody Museum of American Archaeology and Ethnology, Harvard University, Cambridge, Massachusetts

HODGE, F. W.

1920 *Hawikuh Bonework, Indian Notes and Monographs,* Vol. III, No. 3, pp. 130–131; 142 and Pl. XLIX. Heye Foundation, New York

HONEA, KENNETH

1965 *Early Man Projectile Points in the Southwest.* Museum of New Mexico Press, Pamphlet No. 4, Santa Fe, New Mexico

KIDDER, ALFRED V. and GUERNSEY, SAMUEL J.

1919 *Archaeological Exploration in Northeast Arizona,* Smithsonian Institution, Bureau of American Ethnology. Bulletin No. 65, pp. 94–147; pp. 50–51, 60, 70, 73, and Figs. 22, 26, and Pl. 21a. Government Printing Office, Washington, D. C.

KIDDER, ALFRED V.

1932 *The Artifacts of Pecos*, pp. 240–241, and Fig. 201; pp. 195–270. Phillips Academy, by Yale University Press, New Haven, Connecticut

LINDSAY, ALEXANDER, JR.; AMBLER, J. RICHARD; STEIN, MARY ANNE; and HOBLER, PHILIP M.

1968 *Survey and Excavation North and East of Navajo Mountain, Utah, 1959–1962.* Sand Dune Cave. NA7323, pp. 55, 61–63, and 66–69; also pp. 78–79, 80–102, 64–65 (atlatl); pp. 65–67 (atlatl dart); and p. 67 and Fig. 42 (bunt). Bulletin No. 45, Glen Canyon Ser. No. 8, Northern Arizona Society of Science and Art, Inc., Flagstaff, Arizona

MARTIN, PAUL S.; RINALDO, JOHN B.; and LONGACRE, WILLIAM A.

1961 *Mineral Creek Site and Hooper Ranch Pueblo — Eastern Arizona*, Vol. 52, p. 89 and Fig. 63, p. 96 and Fig. 69. Chicago Natural History Museum, Chicago, Illinois

MICHELS, JOSEPH W.

1973 *Dating Methods in Archaeology.* A Volume in the Studies in Archaeology Series. Seminar Press, 111 5th Avenue, New York, New York 10003

MILES, CHARLES

1963 *Indian and Eskimo Artifacts of North America.* Bonanza Books, New York

MORSS, NOEL

1954 *Clay Figurines of the American Southwest.* Peabody Museum of American Archaeology and Ethnology, Harvard University, Cambridge, Massachusetts

PEARL, RICHARD M.

1970 *Rocks and Minerals.* Barnes and Noble, Inc., New York

PECKHAM, STEWART

1965 *Prehistoric Weapons in the Southwest.* pp. 3–6 and Fig. 1 (atlatl); pp. 6–8 and Fig. 4 (arrow). Museum of New Mexico Press, Santa Fe, New Mexico

POGUE, JOSEPH E.

1972 *Turquois* — Memoirs of the National Academy of Sciences, Vol. XII, Part II. The Rio Grande Press, Inc., Glorieta, New Mexico

123

ROGERS, MALCOLM J.

1966 *Ancient Hunters of the Far West* — (Desert Varnish, p. 35, 136–137). Union-Tribune Publishing Co., San Diego, California

RUSSELL, VIRGIL Y.

1957 *Indian Artifacts.* Johnson Publishing Co., Boulder, Colorado

SCHLEGEL, DOROTHY M.

1957 *Gem Stones of the United States.* Geological Survey Bulletin 1042-G, p. 219, United States Government Printing Office, Washington, D. C.

SMILEY, TERAH L.; STUBBS, STANLEY A.; and BANNISTER, BRYANT

1953 *A Foundation for the Dating of Some Late Archaeological Sites in the Rio Grande Area, New Mexico,* Laboratory of Tree-Ring Research, Bulletin No. 6, Vol. XXIX, No. 3. University of Arizona, Tucson, Arizona

SMITH, WATSON

1952 *Excavation of Big Hawk Valley, Wupatki National Monument, Arizona.* Northern Arizona Society of Science and Art, Inc., Flagstaff, Arizona

SPICER, EDWARD H., and CAYWOOD, LOUIS P.

1936 *Two Pueblo Ruins in West Central Arizona.* Social Science Bulletin No. 10, University of Arizona Press, Tucson, Arizona

SWITZER, RONALD R.

1969 *Tobacco, Pipes, and Cigarettes of the Prehistoric Southwest.* Special Report No. 8, El Paso Archaeological Society, Inc., El Paso, Texas

WEBB, TOM

1961 *Bone Musical Instruments,* Educational Series, Paper No. 5. Lea County Archaeological Society, Hobbs, New Mexico

ZIM, HERBERT S., and SHAFFER, PAUL R.

1964 *Rocks and Minerals.* Golden Press, New York

CONTRIBUTORS

Illustrator and Photo Retoucher
Konrad Vaeth

Photography
Joan E. Barnett (black and white)

All black and white photographs (with the exception of those noted as having been taken by museum staff photographers or specified individuals) were shot with a Polaroid CU-5 camera using Type 107 Film for close ups, and a Polaroid 110B camera using Type 42 Film for large artifacts and distance field shots.

Lillian S. Blyth (color)

All color photographs and photographs of photos from publications (black and white) were shot with a Canon Pellix camera with a Macro Canon Lens F1 50 mm *f*/3.5 using Kodak Ektachrome-X Film.

Initial Layout
Franklin Barnett

CONTRIBUTORS

The following listed museums and individuals kindly granted the author permission to use photographs of selected artifacts from their collections. The artifacts which are noted and pictured from museums were permitted through the courtesy of the respective museum directors as indicated. Photos from archaeological publications were selected for inclusion because of their scarcity. The artifacts which are noted and pictured as being from individuals' private prehistoric Indian artifact collections, were all, without exception, recovered from privately owned and held patented lands.

The Arabic numerals before the *Museums, Publication Credits,* and *Individuals* listed below correspond to the number under certain pictured artifacts within this publication, and thus identify the material in the possession of that museum or person. Pictured artifacts which do not show a number are from the author's private collection.

Museums

1. Arizona State Museum, University of Arizona, Tucson, Arizona; Mr. Edwin N. Ferdon, Jr., Director. Photographs of selected Museum material, except as otherwise indicated, were taken by Arizona State Musuem Staff Photographer, Helga Teiwes (Mrs. Stuart French).

2. Desert Caballeros Western Museum, Wickenburg, Arizona; Mrs. Orpha Baker, Director.

3. Museum of Northern Arizona, Flagstaff, Arizona; Dr. Edward B. Danson, Director. Photographs of selected Museum material, except as otherwise indicated, were taken by Museum of Northern Arizona Staff Photographer, Marc Gaede.

4. The Amerind Foundation, Inc., Dragoon, Arizona; Dr. Charles C. Di Peso, Director.

125

Publication Credits

Credits recognized and extended under this category cover photographs of artifacts which were taken from and referenced to the specific archaeological publications listed below. The photographic work was done by Mrs. Lillian S. Blyth. A complete listing of publications from which resumés of other textual material are referenced is found in "Text Reference Material" under ADDITIONAL REFERENCE MATERIAL (pp. 121–124).

5. *Ancient Mimbrenos, Mattocks Ruin, Mimbres Valley, New Mexico,* by Paul H. Nesbitt (pp. 87–89 and Pl. 38, *Geod Rattle*). Published 1931 by the Logan Museum, Beloit College, Beloit, Wisconsin.

6. *Antiquities of the Mesa Verde National Park — Cliff Palace,* by Jesse W. Fewkes (p. 72 and Pl. 28, *Pottery Rest*; and Pl. 27, *Pitch Balls*). Published 1911 by the Smithsonian Institution, Bureau of American Ethnology, Bulletin No. 51, Government Printing Office, Washington, D. C.

7. *Antiquities of the Mesa Verde National Park — Spruce-Tree House,* by Jesse W. Fewkes (pp. 50–51 and Fig. 36, *Hoop*). Published 1909 by the Smithsonian Institution, Bureau of American Ethnology, Bulletin No. 41, Government Printing Office, Washington, D. C.

8. *Archaeological Exploration in Northeastern Arizona,* by Alfred V. Kidder and Samuel J. Guernsey (p. 120 and Pl. 48, *Seed Beater*; and Pl. 60 and 61, and pp. 145–146, *Sunflower*; pp. 50–51, 60, 70, 73, and Figs. 22, 26, and Pl. 21a, *Loom Anchor*). Published 1919 by the Smithsonian Institution, Bureau of American Ethnology, Bulletin No. 65, Government Printing Office, Washington, D. C.

9. *Excavation of Pindi Pueblo, New Mexico,* by Stanley A. Stubbs and W. S. Stallings, Jr. (pp. 121–122 and Pl. 27, *Lightning Stones*). Published 1953 by the School of American Research, Monograph No. 18, Santa Fe, New Mexico.

10. *Excavations in the Chama Valley, New Mexico,* by J. A. Jeancon (p. 26 and Pl. 27, *Bone Breastplate*; p. 64 and Pl. 50, *Gorget*; and p. 67 and Pl. 59, *Koshare Symbol*). Published 1923 by the Smithsonian Institution, Bureau of American Ethnology, Bulletin No. 81, Government Printing Office, Washington, D. C.

11. *Hawikuh Bonework,* by F. W. Hodge (p. 142 and Pl. XLIX, *Game Bones*). Published 1920 by the Museum of the American Indian, Heye Foundation, Vol. III, No. 3, New York.

12. *Material Culture of Pueblo Bonito,* by Neil M. Judd (pp. 276–278 and Pl. 79, *Cedar-Bark Torches* and *Bundles*). Published 1954 by the Smithsonian Institution, Bureau of American Ethnology, Vol. 124, Government Printing Office, Washington, D. C.

13. *Material Culture of Pueblo II in the San Francisco Mountains, Arizona,* by Katharine Bartlett, (pp. 39–40 and Fig. 30, *Medicine Box*). Published 1934 by the Museum of Northern Arizona, Bulletin No. 7, Flagstaff, Arizona.

14. *Paa-ko — Archaeological Chronicle of an Indian Village in North Central New Mexico,* by Marjorie F. Lambert (p. 146 and Pl. XXXV-B, *Cradle Board Toy*). Published 1954 by the School of American Research, Monograph No. 19, Santa Fe, New Mexico.

15. *Survey and Excavations North and East of Navajo Mountain, Utah, 1959–1962,* by Alexander J. Lindsay, Jr., J. Richard Ambler, Mary Anne Stein, and Philip M. Hobler (p. 67 and Fig. 42, *Dart Bunt*). Published 1968 by the Northern Arizona Society of Science and Art, Inc., Bulletin No. 45, Glen Canyon Series No. 8, Flagstaff, Arizona.

16. *Village of the Great Kivas on the Zuni Reservation, New Mexico,* by Frank H. H. Roberts, Jr. (p. 144 and Pl. 56, *Sipapu*). Published 1932 by the Smithsonian Institutuion, Bureau of American Ethnology, Bulletin 111, Government Printing Office, Washington, D. C.

17. Mr. and Mrs. Calvin Armstrong
    Quemado, New Mexico
18. Mr. and Mrs. Jake Armstrong
    Quemado, New Mexico
19. Mrs. Orpha Baker
    Wickenburg, Arizona
20. Mrs. Otto D. Baker
    Wickenburg, Arizona
21. Mr. and Mrs. Lee BeDillon
    Casa Grande, Arizona
22. Mr. and Mrs. Richard A. Bice
    Albuquerque, New Mexico
23. Dr. and Mrs. Edward Bunney
    Wickenburg, Arizona
24. Mrs. Emilia T. Chavez
    Quemado, New Mexico
25. Mr. Milt Coggins, Jr.
    Phoenix, Arizona
26. Mr. and Mrs. Richard K. Cooke
    Wickenburg, Arizona
27. Mr. and Mrs. Jerry Crone
    Quemado, New Mexico
28. Dr. John Glass
    Phoenix, Arizona
29. Dr. and Mrs. Ted A. Glass
    Phoenix, Arizona
30. Mr. and Mrs. Frank Goddard
    Camp Verde, Arizona
31. Mr. and Mrs. Clarence H. Grant, Jr.
    Prescott, Arizona
32. Mr. Daniel Hemerka
    Tucson, Arizona
33. Mr. and Mrs. Ernest Hershberger
    Casa Grande, Arizona
34. Dr. and Mrs. Forrest H. Hill
    Phoenix, Arizona
35. Mr. and Mrs. William E. Hinkley
    Phoenix, Arizona
36. Mr. S. W. Jaques (Estate of)
    Showlow, Arizona
37. Mr. and Mrs. George A. Kalberg
    Quemado, New Mexico
38. Mr. Bill Kish, Phoenix, Arizona
39. Mr. and Mrs. Tom L. Larsen
    Phoenix, Arizona
40. Mr. and Mrs. T. A. Martin
    Phoenix, Arizona
41. Mr. and Mrs. Jerome T. Mason
    Albuquerque, New Mexico
42. Mr. and Mrs. Harvey McCracken
    Camp Verde, Arizona
43. Judge and Mrs. Jack L. Ogg
    Prescott, Arizona
44. Mr. and Mrs. Jeffrey S. Ogg
    Prescott, Arizona
45. Dr. William F. Osborn
    Paradise Valley, Arizona
46. Mr. and Mrs. Glenn E. Quick, Sr.
    Phoenix, Arizona
47. Mr. and Mrs. Ralph Reid
    Camp Verde, Arizona
48. Mr. Thomas W. Simmons
    Tonto Basin, Arizona
49. Ruth G. Sparks, Prescott, Arizona
50. Mr. James H. Swanson
    Phoenix, Arizona
51. Mr. and Mrs. Merlyn Talbot
    Camp Verde, Arizona
52. Mr. and Mrs. Jerry Thompson
    Quemado, New Mexico
53. Mr. and Mrs. Rodney P. Tidwell
    Mesa, Arizona
54. Mr. and Mrs. Frank O. Vernon
    Albuquerque, New Mexico
55. Mrs. Ethel Walters
    Wickenburg, Arizona
56. Mr. and Mrs. Hedekin Whitley
    Quemado, New Mexico
57. Mr. and Mrs. Herman L. Womack
    Prescott, Arizona

ABOUT
THE AUTHOR

Franklin Barnett is a writer — one whose writing abilities, much like his vocations, have led him to be the author of works ranging from creative to various phases of technical writing.

Franklin Barnett left home in Chicago at a very early age, joined the Army, and was stationed in Denver. He was educated at the Polytechnic College of Engineering, Oakland, California. In 1934 he was commissioned a 2nd Lieutenant in the Infantry.

During the next seven years, Mr. Barnett worked in Colorado and California as a surveyman, design draftsman, assistant mine superintendent, free-lance commercial artist, designer for steel fabrication, lighting fixtures, and dwellings.

At the start of World War II, Mr. Barnett resumed his active Army status, and transferred to the Corps of Engineers. Injured in New Guinea while serving as a Company Officer with the 3rd Amphibian Engineer Brigade, 6th Army, he was medically discharged in 1945 with a total permanent disability.

He re-entered the field of architectural design and technical writing. During this period he did considerable philatelic research and writing, and between 1949 and 1964 entered major philatelic exhibitions throughout the country, for which

129

he received many Grand Awards, Best in Show, and so on. Mr. Barnett was a technical writer and supervisor of technical writers with Sandia Laboratory in Albuquerque, New Mexico, from 1950 to 1965, when he retired and moved to Prescott, Arizona.

In 1954, after a period of "rock hounding," Mr. Barnett and his wife, Joan, started surface hunting for Indian artifacts in their spare time. Soon realizing that there was little to be learned, and not much to be gained from this approach to archaeology, the Barnetts started to develop a library of Southwestern archaeological and associated books. As their library material grew, so did their knowledge of archaeology. In this way, and in lieu of a formal archaeological education, a deep appreciation of the profession was built. For many years, study was a nightly affair, while exploration and excavation of prehistoric sites on patented lands became the order of each weekend.

The first excavation by the Barnetts was in September, 1959, and continued, intermittently, in New Mexico, Colorado, and Arizona until the present time.

"Retirement" for Mr. Barnett was merely a word. Since that time he and his wife have excavated several entire prehistoric Indian ruins, and Mr. Barnett authored a number of reports, which have been published, on these excavations. In 1967, the author also wrote the biography of a Yavapai Indian Chieftess, entitled, *Viola Jimulla: The Indian Chieftess,* which has been through three printings.

Mr. Barnett is an Associate of the Northern Arizona Society of Science and Art, Inc., and is a member of the following societies and organizations:

Northern Arizona Society of Science and Art, Inc., Flagstaff

Arizona Archaeological and Historical Society, Tucson

The Albuquerque Archaeological Society, Albuquerque

School of American Research, Santa Fe

Sharlot Hall Historical Society, Prescott

The Westerners, Prescott Corral, Prescott

Life Member, National Disabled American Veterans

The idea for a dictionary of this kind came in the fall of 1971, while completing the excavation of the main Pueblo at Fitzmaurice ruin east of Prescott, Arizona. The author being a firm believer in solid facts, the existence of the many controversies and inconsistencies in archaeological subjects, nomenclature, and vagaries uncovered during the study of countless archaeological reports were contributing factors to the writing of a book of this sort. In writing this Dictionary, practically every field of endeavor with which the author has been associated with through the years was called upon.

With the hope of some small contribution to the unification of at least some of the subject matter of a few of the many ramifications of archaeology, this book is respectfully offered to the profession for whatever purpose it may serve.

130